Hiding in Plain Sight

To Colleen

Ordering Information: Quantity sales and special discounts are available on quantity purchases by corporations, associations, and others. For details, contact the author at the email address above.

Edited by: Heather B. Habelka
Cover design by: Ksenia S.
Cover photo by: Christine Petit of Le Petit Studio
Printed in the United States of America.

Library of Congress Control Number: In progress
First edition, October 2017.

The information contained within this book is strictly for informational purposes. The material may include information, products, or services by third parties. As such, the Author does not assume responsibility or liability for any third party material or opinions. Readers are advised to do their own due diligence when it comes to making decisions.

Hiding in Plain Sight by Sarah Gallardo depicts a real and chilling portrayal of how domestic violence does not discriminate and manifests itself in the most unexpected ways and places.

This true story provides an authentic depiction of one woman's journey through DV and its devastating emotional, physical, mental and spiritual effects on an individual. Beyond the negative experience that this woman endures through this disgusting act of human cruelty, through the tears, anger, cuts and bruises, this woman demonstrates the power of hope through her heroic courage and strength to come out on the other side.

Instead of succumbing to a life of anger, defeat and lack of self-confidence, Ms. Gallardo demonstrates her leadership, her dedication to combatting the DV epidemic and the ability to empower other victims of this horrible crime to speak up- loud and proud. Beyond the wonderful non-profit organization Sarah has created called "Sarah Speaks Up", she has created a following- a tribe- of others who gravitate to her bravery through telling this story of hiding in plain sight.

This story will serve as a guiding light to many – whether they are able and willing to share their story or suffering in silence. It is a story of hope, survival and true human bravery with extraordinary leadership and resilience at its core.

~ Morgan Ferrarott - Board Member, Sarah Speaks Up

Hiding in Plain Sight

A Glimpse Inside the Reality of Domestic Violence

By

Sarah Gallardo

The stories in this book have been written from the author's recollections. They are not written to represent word-for-word transcripts of conversations or events. Rather, the author has retold them in a way that evokes the feeling and meaning of what was said. In all instances the essence of the dialogue is accurate. However, names and identifying details have been changed to protect the privacy of the people involved.

Dedication

To those who have experienced domestic violence- I see you.

I know what you're feeling.

Your situation is not hopeless even though it might feel like it is.

You deserve a happy, healthy life free of abuse.

Planning ahead with a trained professional could be the key to a safe escape and a new life.

Call the National DV Hotline for referrals to services in your area: 1-800-799-7233

There is help. There is hope.

Your children, family, and friends need you.

Please reach out. Please speak up. Please stay safe.

Acknowledgments

To Avalese: You saved my life by giving me a reason to keep living when I had lost all hope. You brought joy and laughter back into my world and remind me (even now) to have fun. You are bright, artistic, generous, smart, funny, kind, and beautiful inside and out. You're my most special Lulu and I love you to the moon and back times infinity no take-backs!

To Sam: You cared enough to call me out when I was detached and stayed when I began to experience the onslaught of emotions waiting behind my walls. You gave me a reason to feel again and a safe space to do it. You deal with my nightmares, triggers, emotional ups and downs, and have more patience with me than I do with myself. You have taught me what love is supposed to feel like and gave me a reason to believe in it. I can't picture my life without you. You are my partner, my one and only teammate. You're my person and I love you!

To my Family: Thank you for being there when you were and not there when you weren't. Now I understand how sad and frustrating it can be to watch someone being abused and feel helpless to stop it. I'm so happy for the progress we've made individually and as a family. I can only hope that healing, support, and understanding continues to grow. I love you!

To my Board of Directors—Kathleen, Joann, Gordy, Brenda, Morgan, and Sue: Thank you for believing in me and in my mission. Thank you for all your hard work and support. Please know that I consider each and every one of you my family. I couldn't have come this far without you! I know that with your talents and tenacity we will continue to do great work with Sarah Speaks Up. I love you!

To Miss Aijah Downer: You were just the fire I needed to continue writing this book! I can't tell you how grateful I am for that. You came into my life as a volunteer, helping with social media, and supporting fundraising events. I'm so glad to call you my friend today. Your determination to reach your goals is astounding and I applaud all that you do! I love you, girl!

To those who contributed financially to this book: From the bottom of my heart, thank you for believing in me enough to help get me to this point. I couldn't have done it without you. I love you!

To my new family: Thanks for taking me and Ava in and loving us. We love you!

To Jenn and Heather: There are no words to express my love, admiration and gratitude for all you did to help me through the writing process. From the bottom of my heart, thank you.

Contents

FOREWORD

When I first met Sarah, I was at an early morning breakfast fundraiser for a local women's shelter that my husband's Foundation was sponsoring. We attend a lot of these events, and on this particular day I was tired, a little distracted, and focused more on the day ahead than the issue at hand. When Sarah began to read one of her poems, a heart-wrenching piece about what it's like to be the object of abuse and forced to hide the reality of their nightmare from others, I was instantly drawn out of my own head and brought into the moment.

I was captivated. The entire room was silent, reflecting on Sarah's words and the deep, painful implications they had. It was clear this woman had been to hell and back, and was here to help others with her story.

I immediately approached her. I knew I had to know her.

I gave her my card, and we got together a few weeks later to talk about how others could be helped by her story, her leadership, and her courage. As a photographer and former journalist, we planned a photo shoot and interview to highlight the transformation she had undergone over the years—from a scared, abused victim to an empowered woman standing on her own two feet, running her own foundation (Sarah Speaks Up), raising her daughter, and working to help others recover from similar situations.

Throughout the interview she maintained her composure,

sharing her story without an ounce of self-pity—displaying professionalism and pure strength. I was in awe.

The fear, the danger, the isolation, and the pain were evident. But it was also evident that she had been a fighter all along. It is almost as if her life had prepared her for a role that she would accept willingly, sacrificing to make it easier for women in similar situations to find a way out, and know that they're not alone.

My husband's foundation, The Petit Family Foundation, like Sarah Speaks Up, also helps those affected by domestic violence. We have seen many good people who sacrifice their time and energy for others. But Sarah's dedication is unique. The fire in her belly drives her to volunteer her time, yes, but she takes it to another level. She is living her purpose, sharing with others unabashedly the private, personal details of her experience so others will know they are not alone. She counsels and cries with the women she helps, and gives a piece of herself to each one.

Sarah and I have become fast friends. We have supported each other and have a special understanding of each other's circumstances, as I too was a victim of domestic violence. As a child and again in my first marriage, I faced abuse. It changed me. It has given me a feeling of empathy for others in soul-crushing situations. It wasn't something I really shared with others, but as I learned more about Sarah's story I began to realize that staying silent was adding to the problem. It wasn't helping me, and it certainly wasn't helping anyone else.

I am inspired by Sarah. I believe we all have a calling, and that my friend is a shining example of shaking off the bad and leading others toward the greater good. I have watched her struggle personally behind the scenes—facing demons that don't disappear, and listened as she recounted nightmares from her trauma.

Sarah's healing has been propelled forward by this book. It was a difficult undertaking for her, as writing and sharing the trauma she experienced brought it all into the present. She re-experienced these events daily as she processed and dissected them, finding the truth and writing it down. The pain she had suppressed all those years ago reared its ugly head into the present, and it made going about her daily life very difficult.

That's the thing about trauma…its roots run deep, and sometimes it sends out shoots into the deeper recesses of our psyche, that we don't see until we disturb the soil. This book required a lot of digging, and a serious amount of facing the pain of the past that no one ever wants to feel.

But people need advocates. Women need others who *can* speak up *to* speak up…not only for themselves, but for those that must remain silent. We all need to see that we have a big problem with abuse and violence in this world. And if we don't begin to support those who have fallen prey to this, we will all suffer, as the aftershocks of negativity spread throughout our communities.

I'm proud of my friend and her tenacity. I'm proud of her voice. I'm proud to know a woman who has been able to rise above and triumph when it would have been so much easier to stay quiet and keep her head down.

I'm proud of Sarah.

Sarah Speaks Up, and because of that, we all benefit.

Christine Petit
Photographer, Owner of Le Petit Studio, LLC
Burlington, Connecticut

Feeling numb, detached.

It helped me survive so many things.

Like being raped.

Like being beaten.

Like being controlled and manipulated every single day.

Like being shot at.

How did I get here?

I don't even recognize myself anymore.

I feel dead inside…

I feel scared and in pain…

I feel nothing…

A LOVE LETTER

Hi.

I don't *really* know you and you don't *really* know me. And while you'll get to know some of my stories, you still won't really know me after you read this. Few people actually do. I don't think that's the point, though. The point, for me, is to give you a glimpse into the life of someone who has survived domestic violence. But this book is just the tip of the iceberg.

If you know nothing about domestic violence, thank you. Thank you for picking up this book and trying to understand. As you read this, please keep an open mind and a compassionate heart. As you read this you may think you don't know anybody who has experienced abuse. I promise you do. It is statistically impossible for you to live in this world and to never have encountered someone who has been abused. I hope that through my story you'll be able to gain insight and perspective. Please know that we, a community of victims and survivors, need you. We need your love and understanding. We need your help and support. I want you to know how important you are. I want you to know that I'm grateful for you and I love you.

If you've been through it yourself, I'm sorry. I understand where you've been and how you feel. Please know that you are not alone. I know how real PTSD is and that most of us who've survived are suffering in silence every day. I know there are days when you feel crazy, depressed, confused, angry, and guilty. And that there are some days you feel so stuck in the past that you think you'll never get out and move on. Or maybe you've stuffed it so far down that you're able to pretend it never happened. You try to live your life in denial, choosing to be numb and detached because it's the safest way to "live." I've lived each of these days. Please know that you are not alone, that there is help, and that I love you.

If you're currently being abused I want you to know that I understand what you're going through and how you feel. I know that your heart and your head don't always agree. I know that you're just trying to survive each day. That you're struggling to keep it together when there are times you just want to scream and cry. I know that sometimes you actually do. Maybe it happens when you're alone in the car, or in the bathroom, or at work when everyone has left the building. Maybe you cry into a pillow, or even scream at your abuser. But most times you try to keep things quiet, organized, running smoothly, functional. I've walked on the same eggshells you're walking on. I want you to know that it's no way to live. You deserve more, you deserve better. Remember that there is help, and even if you can't feel it, there is hope. Please don't ever give up on yourself. This world needs you, your children need you, your friends and family need you. You are not alone.

Please never forget that I love you,
Sarah

The Introduction

SCOTT AND I were introduced by my neighbor. Despite the fact that we were both in relationships—I was living with my fiancé and he was living with his girlfriend and their children—she insisted that we meet. He was eight years older than me and I was attracted to his confidence and strength.

As soon as I learned he was living with his longtime girlfriend and his children, I refused to date him. But he kept pursuing me so I told his girlfriend. I thought I was doing the right thing by telling her. But she blamed me and attacked me physically. At the time I couldn't understand why she would react like that. Now it makes sense. I'm sure she had been conditioned by him over the years to act that way. This was the perfect dynamic for an abuser: to create discord between two women and then manipulate and lie to them both.

I had no contact with him until years later when they moved in right next door to me. I was living in a three-family apartment on the first floor with my fiancé. They also moved into a three-family apartment on the first floor. We were separated by a driveway. That's how close we were. I tried to keep to myself but I know they recognized me.

Shortly after Scott moved next door, my fiancé and I broke up. Scott had seen my fiancé moving out so he knew I was living alone. He started dropping by. He was nice and he made me laugh. It wasn't long before he broke up with his longtime girlfriend and moved in with me. That was an extremely volatile time for everyone involved.

Our relationship was far from the typical knight in shining armor situation. For a long time there was a huge amount of tension between my place and next-door. His ex-girlfriend had just given birth to their third child. Things happened so quickly—too quickly. I allowed him into my home because I was sad and lonely. So I didn't react much when things started to get out of control.

Don't get me wrong. We did have good moments.

I remember how we used to go to the same restaurant every Friday night and get a prime rib dinner, twin lobsters, loaded baked potatoes, and salad. We would split the meals. It became part of our routine and it very seldom got disrupted.

But for the most part, when we went out it was always his version of fun. We used to go to clubs, bars, and parties. He would intentionally put me in situations where I would be around other guys. This would fuel his jealousy and rage. It very quickly became a cycle of dysfunctional love—if you can call it that—and abuse.

People ask me all the time if I ever loved him and I have to say yes. At one time I did. Now I've come to learn about relationships between empathetic people and narcissistic people. They happen all the time. I tried to help him become a better person because of what he had been through as a child. As a child of parents who battled drug and alcohol addiction, I was very empathetic toward his emotional situation. I tried to get him into counseling. I encouraged him to work a steady job, pay child support, and go to church. I encouraged him to better his life and be there more for his kids.

I tried the best I could to create a family.

What I wish for him now is healing (on good days) and sometimes I wish that he gets hit by a bus (on bad days). But more than anything, I wish for his total absence from my life and from my daughter's life. He is a toxic person. He has brought me so much suffering.

My relationship with him could have cost me my life.

THE PILL

STOPPING BIRTH CONTROL pills was one of his first orders of business.

Later I learned that his newborn baby girl had been born prematurely because he pushed his ex down a flight of stairs while she was pregnant. He told me that he left her. That there was too much drama in their relationship and he had to leave. He moved into my apartment almost immediately. Looking back, I'm sure he never really ended their relationship. I'm sure they were embroiled in their own dysfunctional, violent, and sexual relationship. It was blatantly obvious from the beginning but I couldn't see it for what it was.

I was taking medication at the time, so my memory was hazy and my judgment questionable. I wasn't able to function under the drug-induced cloud of prescription mind numbing "help." I was so sedated that I could make a grocery list, but I couldn't go grocery shopping. I could do laundry but I couldn't wash dishes. I existed in my spacious beautiful old apartment. A human in a box, held captive by pills and ignorance. There was nothing blissful about it.

My apartment had a front porch that faced the road and hanging from the rafters were four beautifully maintained bleeding heart plants. Every morning I would drink my coffee on the porch and water my plants. I loved sitting on the porch because it was close enough to being out in the world, but not quite—an illusion of inclusion. There were two bedrooms, a large eat-in kitchen with a spacious pantry, a carpeted dining room with a china closet set into the wall, and two dark-stained sliding doors that led to the living room. I would spend my time on the fluffy green and maroon plaid couch watching *Jerry Springer* and *Maury*, with no regard for how I was wasting my days.

So I didn't think twice about stopping the birth control. I didn't question his motives. Life was like a movie to me back then. I wasn't exactly present and oftentimes I felt like I was outside looking in. Now I know he wanted something permanent to tie us together.

A friend of his, Joan, moved into my apartment shortly after he did. She was seeing a few of his friends, probably him too, now that I think about it. The meds did their job, though. I didn't know or feel any of it either way.

A few weeks after he moved in I started to feel funny. Joan was a nurse and insisted I take a pregnancy test. She was feeling out of sorts too so we took the tests together. I parked my silver Honda Civic behind Price Rite and we both sat on the edge of our respective car doors and peed on the test sticks. We didn't want to do it at home because we didn't want the guys to know. On the edge of a car door…I know. It's not the nicest of places to take a pregnancy test, but I was used to not-so-nice places, so that's how we did it.

She was not pregnant. I was. And so began the severe abuse.

When I told him the news he was happy and angry all at once. I thought that's what he wanted. I certainly wasn't the one trying for this. That evening, to "celebrate," we went to a club. It was a wild place, like any other club. Lights, music, drinks, scantily clad females, and wannabe tough guys trying to get laid. Once we were in, he disappeared and left me with Joan. She was happy to do the drinking for both of us. As time passed I began to wonder where he went so I got up to look for him. It didn't take long to find him grinding with some girl on the dance floor. In my search for him I also found his ex, the one he had three kids with. She hated me and had threatened me since the beginning. I saw red. Here I was, in this place I didn't want to be, with people I didn't want to be around, in danger because of his ex and blatantly disrespected by him on the day I found out I was pregnant, a thing that HE wanted, not me.

I approached him with a look that could have stopped traffic. He saw me but didn't stop grinding, making full unapologetic eye contact as he didn't miss a beat. I could see the amusement on his face. This was funny to him.

So there I went, sucked straight into the drama, wanting attention and retribution. What did I do? The wrong thing. I should have left. But I didn't. I found a guy who had been looking at me and I proceeded to dance with him. For a while it was fun but the guy was handsy and that was certainly noticed. Scott and I left shortly thereafter, screaming at each other the whole way back. Of course, it was painted as my fault.

It was always my fault.

Being that I was pregnant, I immediately stopped all my medication. But it didn't matter. The lies, violence, drama, cheating, and manipulation got the best of me. The stress and turmoil was too much. The pregnancy did not survive. Looking back, that was the absolute perfect time to leave, cut my relatively few losses and get out. Nope. I was too embroiled in the cycle of control and manipulation, trying to fix, help, and change him. Trying to create happiness out of the shitstorm that was my life, as I had always been trying to do since I was a little girl.

After no longer being pregnant, I was a wreck. Vodka became my best friend. We did everything together. We went to the mall together, went for walks together, we watched TV together, we even passed out on the couch together. It was a blissful relationship that, for a time, took the place of the mind-numbing pills I had been taking for years.

This friendship was not sustainable, however. You know that friend who takes more than they give? That's what happened. It was time, money, and peace of mind wasted. I realized I was trying to numb the pain and it wasn't working. Vodka and I had to part ways.

After concentrating on getting back on track, I decided to venture beyond my place on the couch. I went to school for dog grooming. I chose that profession because I had trouble dealing with people. They had been pretty terrible to me and I took comfort in being surrounded by dogs and cats.

Now off my medication, I lost weight, got some clarity, and could focus once again. And I left Scott.

Gram and my aunt took me in. There was no room for me in the house so they cleared a space in the basement for me, among the piles of dusty chairs and boxes of forgotten things. I was isolated down there. I felt like a refugee. The one person who pursued me during these dark days in the dungeon was Scott. It was easy to mistake his controlling, manipulative ways for love. His tone changed from volatile and angry to one of concern. He missed me. He sent messages, checking in regularly. He seemed to care how I was doing. He became my support while I was trying to leave him. My family didn't know what to do or how else to help. After a month or so I left the safety of the basement and jumped back into the fray. My resolve to stay away from Scott had slowly been whittled to dust.

We moved from my beautiful spacious apartment to a much smaller one around the corner. The landlord was a well-kept man. I'm pretty sure he had OCD. Everything needed to be painstakingly in its place. He was particular about his car, his house, his yard, and even the way he dressed. I could tell he ironed his jeans because there was always a crease in the pant legs. His black New Balance sneakers looked buffed and polished, and his shirts never seemed to wrinkle. He liked us right away. Scott played his usual convincing stand-up guy and loving boyfriend routine and it worked like a charm.

Over time, however, the landlord became suspicious. Because we were living in the same building I'm sure he could hear yelling, banging, and me crying all the time. The landlord was an EMT. One

THE GROCERY STORE

I⟡ DIDN'T MATTER if we went together or if I went alone. The grocery store was a place that gave me severe anxiety. Ironically it used to be the only place that calmed me down.

In the height of my depression, I'd stare down the aisles and feel an overwhelming sense of calm wash over me. Everything was so organized, all in a row, labels facing forward proudly like soldiers displaying their badges of honor. There had been so much chaos and disarray spewed throughout my entire life: a messy house, gross inconsistencies from those who were supposed to be my foundation, infractions, intrusions, excuses, and life-altering trauma. The organization of canned goods and condiments eased my mind. It was the only thing I could count on to be always this way, always what I needed it to be.

Speaking of needs, we all need food, right? Despite how hard I tried to cook the food he liked, he always found fault with me. Even when I'd bring home his favorites or I'd bake him his favorite carrot cake with cream cheese frosting—the same day he demanded it. I learned from my grandmother at a very young age that good home-cooked food was a way to love people. And so I did. I did all the stuff I was "supposed" to do, or at least I thought so.

Scott did give me credit for my ability to shop on a tight budget. I took full advantage of the specials and coupons as often as I could.

I planned and strategized what we needed, largely because we had so little money. I loved showing off how much money I'd saved. I beamed when he'd brag to people about what a thrifty shopper I was. At times he even suggested people come with me so they could "learn from a pro." It's funny the things I held onto, what made me feel appreciated. How I learned to turn the sprinkles of basic human kindness into pillars of love.

When I went by myself he would pay attention to how long it took me and check the receipt when I got home. He'd look at the timestamp at the top and match it to the time I got back, making sure that I didn't take any detours. If he saw on the receipt that I'd been helped by a male cashier, he'd ask why I picked that line and if we flirted with each other. He'd ask if I got his number or gave him mine. There were always accusations.

He was always watching, always keeping tabs, making sure things worked out the way he needed them to. I remember when I was waitressing at night after grooming school. Every day was the same. I'd wake up at six a.m., take out my dogs, eat breakfast (sometimes), get dressed, and go to grooming school. I'd always leave early because I worked fast and because I had to be done in time to go home, shower, and get to my evening waitressing job at the restaurant three blocks down from our apartment. There were nights I'd catch a glimpse of him standing outside the restaurant. He'd watch me interact with people all the while judging, assessing, remembering. "So who was the guy in the red shirt?" he'd ask. "I don't know," I'd say. "Pretty friendly for not knowing him," he'd reply.

One night was different than the rest. This night he came inside the restaurant. He asked to be seated in my section. I brought him rolls, water, a drink, and then came to take his food order. He watched me serve the other people but got off completely on the fact that I waited on him as I did the others. I could tell he liked making me uncomfortable in a place where I could do nothing about it. He wasn't even a nice customer. He was picky. I don't know why this shocked me. It shouldn't have, but it did. I found my blood boiling hotter and hotter every time I went to his table. He sat, so self-assured and smug. He enjoyed every second of it. I, on the other hand, was embarrassed, angry, hurt, and offended. I was seething. It was glaringly obvious that this was the dynamic of our relationship played out in a dinner setting: me serving reluctantly, angrily, but serving nonetheless, him receiving, entitled.

He ordered lobster.

I had introduced him to lobster. He had never eaten it until we met. How lovely that he discovered how much he loved it! How lovely that I had the privilege of serving it to him while I got to eat bread in the kitchen. I just wanted him to leave but he lingered. I imagine he enjoyed the view from the frontline more than the view from outside the window. When he finally made his move to get up from the table he was sure to say goodbye. "You got this, right?" he said, motioned to his finished meal and walked out like a gold plated peacock. He didn't pay for his food. He didn't leave a tip. I used my tip money to pay for the lobster dinner I served him.

THE FALLING

I HAD LOST one pregnancy. Now I was going to lose my second.

The first time, the loss of my pregnancy was a blur. Everything was chaotic. I was actually trying to leave Scott back then. To be honest, I think there was always a part of me that was trying to leave him. He hated that part of me. Despised it, in fact. He knew she was there, that strong, hopeful, independent woman. What better way to clip her wings than a miscarriage? According to him they were my fault; flesh of my flesh that he said I wasn't strong enough to carry.

The stomach pain, that I can only assume was happening because a series of fights, started after I picked him up from work. He was working for a moving company at the time. We'd stopped at a gas station so we weren't far from the hospital. He drove me there instead of getting gas. The ride was silent, and seemed to take forever, even though the hospital was at most five minutes away. I could tell he was nervous. He was holding my hand trying to comfort me. I sank into him. I needed the comfort.

He was warm. I felt safe with him in that moment. It was like he would have protected me from the world if he could, or at least for that car ride to the hospital. I clung desperately to that feeling. I wanted to pause time just so I could feel him treat me so kindly, the way I had always wanted to be treated. He looked at me while he was driving. There was fear in his eyes. Maybe even a glimpse of remorse.

I'm not really sure. He was trying to reassure me, trying to be strong. The truth is that I needed him to be.

The hospital was sterile and cold: white walls, generic pastel prints of flowers, health magazines, downcast people, and the smell of rubbing alcohol. The woman at the desk was kind but hurried. She had olive skin and curly black hair. She looked to be in her mid-fifties. She smelled like a perfume I remembered but couldn't place. She was wearing a blue cardigan with a pin that said, "How can I help you?"

Help? Me? Yes, please! HELP!!!

I filled out my paperwork dutifully and waited, my abdominal area feeling like it was having a seizure.

The hospital staff moved quickly. As we waited for the doctor Scott talked to me. "Everything's gonna be fine. We can get pizza when we go home. What do you want on top? Your pick, whatever you want." His attempts to comfort me felt so foreign but I lapped up every single molecule of every single word. *See? He does love me. He's trying. I know it's been stressful lately but things will get better when the baby's born.*

After all the tests were done, my loving, caring, concerned, supportive, Oscar award-winning man sat next to my bedside hand in hand, as we heard the words, "I'm sorry. There is no heartbeat"

There were more words that followed, "Take your time to process, I'll give you some privacy. We can discuss the options when you're ready." But I had already begun to cry and hyperventilate. This was made worse by the fact that Scott got up angrily and left.

I wasn't expecting the gut-wrenching noise that traveled from the square center counter of the emergency room minutes later, down the hall and into my room. It was like something I heard on the Discovery Channel when a large animal is taken down and eaten, its last cry before death. The raspy howl of a scream was his. Followed by the swiping of his arm across the countertop, hurling files and papers and whatever else was resting there, onto the floor.

I didn't see it happen, I only heard the howl and the doctor's retelling of events. How he warded off the security guards to protect my grief-stricken boyfriend, the sad baby killer.

I couldn't tell the doctor that I was terrified to go home because he would surely blame me. Or that he beat me, belittled me and manipulated me, and that those were the real reasons for our loss. I couldn't breathe. I couldn't talk.

After 4 mg of Ativan I was discharged. I had decided to take the pills that would force my body to dilate and pass the fetus, rather than opting for a D&C, the surgical removal of the fetus. "Pass the fetus," the most clinical words to say, "Force what could have been your baby, but never will, out of your body." I walked out of the sterile sliding doors holding paperwork, my purse, and the hand of the murderer, laughing hysterically from the drugs, and carrying death inside my body.

I didn't take the pills right away. I was too busy waltzing with denial. The dance just left me sick and dizzy, though, and eventually I gave in.

With no idea what to expect, as I had never given birth before, I began the regimen of tablets as prescribed even though the bottle of painkillers, meant to ease the process, had been emptied the day before. I had no idea that labor would be induced, although it may have been explained in detail at the hospital.

Instead of staying home, Scott decided to take a trip to get more pot. Of course, he couldn't leave me by myself. Not out of concern for my well-being, but because he felt the need to monitor me at all times. I was forced to join him.

The pain began on the ride home. It was like being stabbed in the abdomen with hot pokers. Fire and brimstone on four wheels, as we journeyed home, me screaming and writhing in pain the whole time.

Three flights of stairs.

I deserved those three flights of stairs. My feet carried me up to the fourth floor where I walked past the laundry I had hung the night before. Clean flags of Downy freshness swaying in the slight breeze, leading me to the doorway of what would become my second baby's burial ground.

I lay on our bed, still screaming and writhing, wishing I hadn't been such a gluttonous pig with the painkillers. Scott just bustled around trying to come up with some way to fix what was happening. He decided it was best that I sleep through it, so he gave me one of his sleeping pills. I don't know how many milligrams were in the horse pill, and I didn't ask. Obediently, desperately, I swallowed it.

I quickly began to feel woozy and staggered to the bathroom, now leaning on my helpful partner. I sat on the toilet just in time for the gush of blood and black tissue. Four flushes of what looked like only blood and no water. At some point in the purge, it occurred to me that I might be losing too much blood. But my mind was drifting like a cloud, like a wisp of smoke in the wind, it was hardly present in the bathroom with me at all. Somehow I made it to bed as I fell into a forced sleep. I continued to bleed, in my tortured slumber, through my clothes, every blanket, the mattress topper, and onto the mattress itself.

I don't know how long I slept, where Scott was while I did, or how much blood I lost. It is only now, as I write these words, that I realize how lucky I was to wake up.

Two days later was a freestyle concert Scott wanted to go to. I had purchased tickets well in advance. Scott was on a tear that day. I don't remember why, all I can remember is him saying that I was milking the miscarriage for all it was worth, that when it came time for things that were important to him I didn't care enough, and that I was taking too long to get anything done and we'd probably be late because of me.

To placate the 6'1" child in my kitchen, I jumped into the shower for some peace and quiet.

Like a robot I moved the soap over my skin. The bubbles

brought out the smell of Irish Spring, the clean feeling I so desperately wanted but couldn't seem to achieve. I could hear him yelling from the other room while the smell of cigarette smoke and cheap brandy filled the house. I began humming and taking deep breaths while I tried to force my body to relax.

As I did, the true end came.

A sharp cramp and another gush, my instantly cold hands automatically rushed to my mouth to stifle the scream that tried to escape. The trail of blood traipsed down my legs and led to what my eyes were fixated on. I was removed from it, and it from me.

I considered calling Scott in to help but quickly ruled it out. Here I was, stalling, dragging my feet, as he paced, lit cigarette in one hand and half-empty bottle of E & J in the other, waiting impatiently for me to be ready to go to the concert I bought tickets for to make him happy. No. I knew that calling him in was only going to make this unbearable, inhumane thing worse and I couldn't let that happen.

I knew what I had to do. I grabbed a clean brown towel from the rack and put it between my legs. I walked with the smell of Irish Spring and blood still on my skin to get as much toilet paper as I could. I clasped the paper in my hand, the hand that no longer belonged to me. I left myself. The hand reached for the object. I only know the hand picked it up because it was no longer in the tub. I walked to the toilet, dropped it in, and the hand flushed it.

I silently finished my shower, cleaning my body as best I could, got dressed in the baggiest clothes I owned, put a maxi pad in my underwear, tied a sweatshirt around my waist, put a thick folded towel on the drivers seat of my car, and drove to the concert.

We made it there on time.

The Key

I was so excited to finish grooming school. This was me finishing something, pushing through the adversity of my day-to-day life. All the while, I was being pulled deeper into the throes of our dysfunctional relationship. People were noticing and trying to help me, but tentatively. I remember the owner of the grooming school telling me that I could make a good living doing this work but I should leave Scott because he would only drag me down. I'm not sure if he realized that there were times I was literally dragged, but that was only the beginning of me ignoring people's warnings and denying the help they offered. Scott had me like a trained lion at the circus. I danced and jumped through hoops of fire on his command. I forgot what freedom was. I was becoming tame. I was becoming his.

The minute I was able to, I started applying for jobs. I couldn't wait to stop waitressing at night! I was offered an opportunity to groom at and manage a small shop. I remember having a conversation with the owner, telling him that Scott could be present for all our meetings, and that anything he had to say to me he could say in front of him, too. I think the owner liked knowing that I had a man around so if I needed help I wouldn't have to call him all the time. The real reason I included him in all my conversations was because I had to. That was a requirement, just one of the many rules I "lived" by.

After landing the job I felt like I was beginning a new chapter.

Even though it was so small, so far removed from my dream of becoming a singer, I was happy nonetheless. It was a win and I grabbed it with all my strength.

Being at the shop alone was bliss. I began to form a routine. I ran the show there. I was in control.

The shop was a small square building behind a pizza place, at the entrance of an industrial park. I liked it because I was surrounded by people. They were close by, but not too close. The main room of the shop had a wooden counter with a register, phone, appointment book, and a jar of doggie biscuits. The walls were white and clean. There was a small bathroom with a stand-up shower in the back. The main room had a hydraulic table, a Shop-Vac, a tub with shampoos, a washer and dryer for towels, a rolling compartment for all my tools, and a small round table in the corner with four chairs around it. That's where I ate my lunch if I had time. There was a room full of crates and driers off to the side, separated by two soundproof glass doors, a feature I very much appreciated.

I loved being there. I loved the people and, more than anything else, the animals. I began to get comfortable with the area. The people in the industrial park were kind and helpful. It's amazing how much a simple "Good Morning" made me feel welcome and normal, part of life, part of a community, part of something. There was pep in my step when I left our apartment in the morning. I had found a place where I belonged, far away from our bungalow of control.

About six months after I started the job it got cold and snowy. One morning it was so cold that the shop door was frozen shut. I tried to put the key into the knob and turn, as I did every morning, but it wouldn't budge. I was afraid the key would break off in the hole and then I'd really be in trouble so I put my things back in the car, got a book of matches from my glove compartment, and returned to the door. I always arrived early to give myself time to settle in, answer messages, and set up, but I was acutely aware of the fact that people would be arriving with their pets soon.

So here's the scene. You can laugh if you want. As I recall this part, believe me, I'm chuckling too. Me in full winter clothes—hat, scarf, boots, and gloves that had been removed for the task—crouched over, breathing warm air on the doorknob and switching to a lit match, rotating breath with fire and so on. If I had driven by, I'd have wondered what that crazy person was doing, but that's all I had to work with at the time and the clock was ticking. After a few rotations of warmth, I tried the key and as I did the phone inside the shop rang.

Great. Missing calls already. Come on, Sarah, focus.

I tried the door again. No luck. Back to breathing and matches. The phone rang again.

Who's canceling because of the snow?

I was about to approach one of the guys from the auto body shop who had just pulled into his usual spot, when the phone rang again. It stopped and rang again. And again. And again. This time there was a message being left on the answering machine that I could hear on the other side of the door.

"Yo. You're real funny, you know that. Where the fuck you at? You been stopping on the way to work? Bitch, who the fuck you with?" and the message ended. I stood there dumbfounded. The phone rang again immediately. "Bitch, you think this is a joke? I ain't playin' with you. Answer the fucking phone. NOW!" The phone rang again. "I'm on my way." Click.

I couldn't open the door, customers would be arriving any minute, and he was on his way. Irate. I went to the car and looked around for anything else to help solve this snowballing problem. I discovered that he had been calling and messaging my cell phone. He had timed out my drive to work and would contact me when I got there. I forgot about the phone. I left it in the car so it wouldn't get all snowy. The price for that mistake? I didn't know, but I knew I would soon find out. I was trapped. If I unlocked the door and he arrived afterward, he wouldn't have proof that I was locked out. If I waited for him to show up, customers would witness his rage. I couldn't have that. I tried one more time to open the door by myself. I couldn't ask the other guy for help now. If Scott showed up while there was another man present he'd instantly think I was cheating with him, and we'd both get it…all at my precious shop, my peace away from chaos, the one place I felt safe and free. I tried to call back from my cell phone but he didn't answer. I knew he was on his way.

Maybe it was the sun coming up, maybe it was a one degree change in temperature, or maybe all the breathing and tiny flames paid off, but the next time I tried the door finally unlocked. Just in time for my first customer. Then another. The third car to pull into the parking lot belonged to his friend. Scott got out, slammed the door, and approached the shop as the car drove away. As he was approaching another customer arrived. He held the door as she walked in with her dog. He was pleasant, charming and funny. He pet her dog and helped bring him into the back. He acted as if he belonged there and didn't bat an eye. The customer left and he didn't say a word to me. He just turned and sat at the round table in the corner of the shop. He stayed there all day, sitting while I worked. He nodded off a few times and I caught myself thinking I could just slit his throat with my scissors or call the cops or run or scream or hide…but I didn't do any of those things. I finished my work. The tension was more than I could take, all day spent wondering what he was going to do and when it was going to happen, how bad it would be and how long it would take for me to recover.

When the last dog was picked up I began to clean, as I did every day. I got halfway through and had to use the bathroom. By this time he woke up and started yelling at me, accusations, name-calling, questions that I had already answered… I knew nothing I said would make it better. And to be honest, there were times I'd lie, eventually giving in to his accusations because it was easier than telling the truth. He didn't believe me anyway and he was unrelenting until I admitted that what he was saying was true. It wasn't. I didn't do what he said, but he was nicer when he forgave me for what I didn't do.

As I went around the corner he rushed up behind me and pushed me into the bathroom. I fell forward into the small standup shower and tried to regain my balance as he locked the door. There was pain and ringing. He had hit my right ear and the side of my face as I was trying to stand up. The force knocked me down. I was on my hands and knees. My right hand instantly went to my ear. It was hot and the ringing noise was deafening. He was still yelling but the sound was muffled:

"Stupid bitch

Whore

Piece of shit

Liar

Cheater

Lazy cunt"

I was stuck in the corner of a little shop that stood on its own, behind a pizza place in an industrial park where other people were closing up for the day.

I was trapped.

I tried to move forward, out of the shower, but he wouldn't move. He pushed me and I bumped the back of my head. "Let me out," I said, voice shaking. "Fuck you, stupid bitch! You can come out when I say," as he hit his own chest like an ape. "Let me out!" I screamed and pushed him back into the bathroom door. It was a fight now. I wasn't going to stay in the shower and let him beat on me. As he was about to come back at me, I moved to the side with my back to the wall, got my hand on the door and unlocked it as another right punch landed on my right ear, knocking the left side of my head into the doorframe.

Ringing. Blood. Pain.

I ran toward my tools. They were still out on the table, as I hadn't finished cleaning up yet. I grabbed my scissors and pointed them at him as he quickly approached. He stopped. There was a moment suspended between us. He looked at me. I can't imagine what was going on in his mind but all I could think of was how is this going to end. I didn't know what I was planning to do with the scissors. They were the first weapon I could think of that was nearby. I suppose I would have cut him, if I had to, if he kept hurting me. But instead I turned them on myself. He stood in front of me and watched as I held the scissors in my right hand and cut my left forearm repeatedly. At least ten times, some cuts deeper than others. "Is this what you want?" I screamed hysterically as tears rolled down my face and blood rolled down my arm and dripped onto the floor. "You wanna kill me? Cuz I don't care anymore!" I started to hyperventilate. It was true. I didn't care. I couldn't. It hurt too much.

His face turned from anger to fear. He approached me, took the scissors out of my sweaty clenched fist, put them down, and hugged me. My blood was all over me, on the floor and now on him. He found a clean towel and wrapped my arm, called one of his friends and told him I was cutting myself and asked him to come help. This story, as told to the friend, started and ended there. The part leading up to the self-slit forearm was left out. I was deemed mentally unstable and that was that. I needed help. Me. I was the problem.

The guys were kind enough to clean up all my blood, except for the bit on the doorframe that no one else saw. They ordered a pizza, got a six-pack of beer, and the three of us ate at the round table in the corner, me with a wrapped forearm. The rest of the night Scott was nice to me, doting even. He was helpful and he didn't yell. He put his arm around my shoulder and held my hand. In that moment, he was everything I wished for. All I wanted was for someone to love me, to be kind to me, to support and care for me. For a short time he did that. But the cuts healed, leaving one scar, and the incident was forgotten. The tenderness faded. The care and concern I had paid for with my own blood vanished and we were back to "normal" in no time.

After that incident, he came to work with me every day. He sat in the corner of the shop. He watched my every move and he listened to my every word. He did what any concerned partner would do for someone they love who is obviously mentally unstable. Right? And so my oasis slipped away, all because of a frozen doorknob.

The Shot

It was a typical summer night.

We were making the rounds, stopping from bar to bar so Scott could make his sales. At that time I didn't have to try to fit in. I was no longer the high school diving team captain who was accepted to Berklee College of Music. I was a Spanish-speaking ghetto chick. My disguise fooled them all. Most importantly I fooled myself. I fit in so well that even my normal English speaking voice had a Spanish accent. All part and parcel of the chameleon's smoke and mirrors.

The tightrope walk of getting dressed had gone without a hitch. I had to look cool, current, but not too hot. No clothes too tight or too revealing. Otherwise I would have been asking for other men to look at me. Skirts and dresses had to be below the knee and loose fitting. He preferred me to wear an oversize T-shirt and hoodie with baggy pants and sneakers or boots. That's not my style. It never was. But I wasn't in charge of my wardrobe. I was expected to dress to please him and only him.

We got out of the car and walked into the bar. Through the heavy glass doorway, I was greeted with the smell of stale beer and bleach. The setup was interesting. It reminded me of an Irish pub but it was usually full of mostly Hispanic people. There were huge mirrors on the wall behind the bar where all the liquor was. A few photos of the owner and staff at holiday parties were taped onto the glass. The bar was long and there was only walking space between the barstools and the wall. The top half of the walls were painted forest green and the bottom half was dark brown wood paneling. I always loved the textured ceiling tiles in that bar. It reminded me of one of those home makeover shows. I was sure most people didn't notice that because the ceilings were so high, but I spent a lot of time there trying to be somewhere else so I'd look around a lot. Two doorways led to the adjacent room, which was much bigger and had three pool tables and a small dance floor. The red carpet had seen better days but nobody seemed to notice that either. The jukebox was usually playing Reggaeton. The smell of cigarette smoke and pot drifted in through the back door from the people hanging out on the deck.

I wasn't comfortable there. Truth be told, I wasn't comfortable anywhere.

Scott ordered drinks for us and entered the poolroom with me close behind. He walked with a confident swagger. There was an air of arrogance about him. The posture he presented to the world was that of an alpha, but volatile, ready to keep what was his and take what was yours if he wanted it. As we walked into the room, he stopped short. I followed suit, or else I would have bumped into him. With an inflated ego he raised both hands to address the crowd.

His New York accent carried from one corner of the room to the other.

"Just so we're clear, she's with me. Nobody talks to her without my permission or you'll get popped in the mouth."

Some people stopped what they were doing and stared in what looked like disbelief. Others gave one quick nod of acceptance and went on with their game. I felt like I was going to cry or vomit but I kept a straight face. Better to feel nothing than to feel embarrassment and humiliation. I was his property. At that point, I could have been his duffel bag.

I had flipped the switch. That switch inside me that I love so much, that's kept me from feeling more of my life than I actually ever have. No more knot. No more tears. No more nausea. No more embarrassment and humiliation. I was at home in my numbness.

Scott approached a guy he knew. They exchanged some words I couldn't hear and then he motioned to me. "Play a couple games with my boy, I'll be around," he directed. He turned to his friend and said, "Watch her for me." He smacked my butt and walked away.

This was never good. Either way, I was bound to lose. "I'll be around" meant "I'll be watching you." "Watch her for me," meant "If anything goes wrong I'm holding you responsible."

The guy he chose for me to play pool with seemed to understand fully what this meant. He appeared to be no stranger to the streets. I'm sure he could have held his own. He was wearing a baggy red T-shirt and a matching red hat. His jeans were baggy and blue. They draped perfectly over his crisp clean work boots. It occurred to me that he probably didn't do much work in them. He had a gold chain with Jesus' head hanging in the center. His big square rhinestone earring was obnoxious. I noticed that his hands were clean and his fingernails were well maintained, another indicator that he probably didn't work much. The only blemish was a cigarette stain on his right hand. He had the same kind of stain on his teeth. He appeared to be very confident. I've come to realize that whether you are actually confident or not, in the streets you have to act like you are or you'll be eaten alive. His name was Pedro.

I can only assume he was given permission to talk to me because he asked, "Your break or mine?" I think he was trying to be nice, but I quickly remembered our situation. I answered, "Your table, you break." And so he did.

He was good. I could tell he had been playing for a long time. But deep down I knew that no matter what happened this night wasn't going to end well. If I won the game Scott would come back over and gloat. On the ride home he'd accuse me of flirting with the guy, ask if I got his number, take my phone, go through it and, no matter what he found, smash it on the ground. If I lost the game, he'd come back over and ridicule me in front of everybody. He'd act disgusted and most likely leave without telling me, to do what and with whom, I never knew. Then he'd show back up ready to leave, probably high or having been with another woman, disgusted to have to come back to me. The ride home would be scary. I'd be accused of talking to other guys while he was gone, even though I'm sure he'd assigned me several "babysitters." As Pedro did better, he drank more. As he drank more, he got bolder. He started mouthing off to me, maybe as a tactic to get me flustered. This was definitely the opposite of flirting, or so I thought. I lost the game.

Scott walked in as Pedro was making some comment about how bad I was at pool. Instead of saying something to him he turned to me, "You gonna let him talk to you like that?" he asked. (The irony here is too much for me. Just sayin'.) There was no right way for me to handle any situation. I'd be wrong no matter what I did. If I stood up to the guy, I'd be bold and disrespectful. If I stayed quiet I was allowing myself, his property, to be disrespected. It was always lose-lose.

He turned to the guy, "Yo! That's my wife! You gonna disrespect my wife in front of my face?" We weren't married at the time, but he still called me his wife. Pedro apologized and backed off. Scott had made his alpha stance known. He turned around. "Come on, Ma," he said. And out the door, into the car we went.

As I knew would happen, he started yelling at me about allowing myself to be disrespected. This wasn't my first rodeo, so I figured I'd turn the tables. It was the only way I'd have a chance at avoiding getting hit when we got home. I told him it was his fault for making me play pool with that guy in the first place, and how could HE allow ME to be disrespected like that? I tried to keep talking so I could make my point clear and not give him a chance to retaliate. If I could win this verbal argument, I might actually be able to avoid the physical one that usually happened afterward.

Maybe I had a good argument. Maybe I actually made sense to

him. Maybe none of it mattered and he was going to do what he was going to do no matter what. Either way, I was scared. When things like this would happen I started to feel cold and clammy. My reactions were slow and didn't always make sense. He would leave me in a state of never knowing what was going to happen next. It was unnerving. I was terrified. I was confused. I spent most of my time like a deer in headlights, trying to scramble out of the way but not knowing which way to go.

He dropped me off at home and left the car. He told me to go into the house and said that he'd be back later. He left walking but I have a feeling he got a ride. Later I found out that he went back to the bar and pulled a gun on Pedro. He didn't shoot him, but he threatened him. The bar had it on video with no audio. I don't know if they called the police but he was banned from that bar after the incident.

I didn't know he had a gun.

I became concerned about where he went, and what he was up to, so I decided to drive around and look for him. This was an all too familiar wild goose chase. I couldn't find him at any of his usual places and I was getting tired, so I decided to just go home and wait for him to come back.

The back yard where we lived was small. It was encased by a chain link fence. There was enough space for three cars to park. I remember thinking how nice it was to be out there alone. It felt strange to feel normal in that moment. The knot in my stomach seemed to loosen a bit. The sky was clear and pitch black, but for the flecks of light the stars gave off. It was beautiful and so very peaceful.

I had parked my car in the usual spot. The tree branches swayed in the slight breeze. It was late at night and pretty quiet. I remember taking the keys out of the ignition and grabbing my cell phone, thinking how cool it was that it didn't get broken. I assumed that I would be sleeping before he got home. I was happy he was out and I could get to bed peacefully.

As I moved toward the apartment door I saw a figure in the dark. I don't know if he was waiting near the bushes, watching me, or if he had just gotten home. I don't know if he walked there or got a ride back. All I know is that he started quietly walking up the driveway toward me.

"Where the fuck were you? You know this is all your fault!" he said.

Before I could answer him he raised his hand. The gun was in it. While walking toward me he shot one time.

I didn't move. There was no time to react.

He shot at me.

He shot at me.

I was breathing. *Am I breathing? Oh my God!*

Eyes wide, holding my breath, hands shaking. Frozen.

My blood seared. I was stuck in the spot where I was standing. I could hear the shattering of glass behind me. The bullet missed me but I don't know by how much. It shattered the window of my car.

He put the gun by his side and said, "I'm sorry I missed you."

With a grimace of disgust he went inside the apartment.

I don't know how long I stood there. I don't know if he meant to shoot me or just scare whatever life I had left out of me. I didn't run. I didn't scream. I didn't call the police.

It wasn't real.

It wasn't real.

Did that really happen? *It couldn't have happened.*

Eventually, like a zombie, like a pig to slaughter, I went inside. I don't remember much else about that night but I know that I went to sleep eventually.

When I woke up the next morning it was business as usual. I got dressed for work and got in my car. The only difference was that I had one less window and I was sitting on broken glass.

THE WEDDING

Scott and I had run out of money and needed food so he brought me to a church he had attended a few times, knowing they had a food pantry. When we went there, everyone was so friendly, generous, and caring—full of love and joy. I felt at home. My childhood had been difficult, and my relationship with my family was strained, so for the first time in a long time I felt like I belonged.

The people ushered us in as he introduced me and explained our situation. They gave us so much food that it filled the car. We were set for a while and a huge amount of stress was lifted from my shoulders.

I loved the feeling of going to church and being around the congregation so much that we began to go every Sunday. Then we started Bible study on Wednesdays. We sang, prayed, worked, and shared the holidays with our church family. The whole church prayed that we'd find an apartment, and we did. The whole church prayed that Scott would get a job, and he did. And when the doctors told us that we'd lost my second pregnancy, the whole church prayed over me.

After the miscarriage I relied on my church family for support and they were there through it all. All the while, I tried to fix our relationship, to change the dysfunctional dynamic, to become a healthy couple. As best I could, anyway. Scott had no interest in that because it would have required him to change. I now know that most abusers are unwilling or incapable of looking at themselves introspectively. They don't see what they have done or are doing wrong. They place blame, looking for new ways to control, manipulate, and mold their victim into whatever they want them to be. He couldn't hold a job, but he was great at this.

Time passed. The abuse flared as did his drug use. The nights were long as I sat at home—wondering where he was or if he'd come home at all. In retrospect I should have been happy when he was out. The nights I spent alone were quiet and peaceful yet I became fixated on how unfair our relationship was. I had to be always accounted for but he could do as he pleased. I couldn't ask too many questions because that would spark his rage so I danced around him, shuffling as softly as possible. Disturbing as little as I could. My suspicions never voiced but swallowed. To say that I had checked out would be an understatement. I denied reality. My brain saw things through a distorted filter.

I was lost.

After he spent a full month's rent money on cocaine, I knew we couldn't keep going. He was sick from the drugs, shaking, sweating, lying in the fetal position, trying to get up but collapsing. I could have walked away then. He couldn't have done anything to stop me. Now that I think about it there were several times I could have left easily but the threat of him finding me loomed. He said he'd track me down, hurt my family, that he'd have me one way or another. So I stayed like a lab rat in an open cage.

I began making calls to rehab facilities—not an easy task. "No beds." "We don't take that insurance." "Full to capacity." "Call back next week." "We'll put him on a waiting list." So much effort put into saving my captor, helping my abuser.

Eventually I found a place that had one bed available but we had to leave immediately and drive an hour to get there. That was it. Bags packed. Out the door. On our way.

The car ride was strange. He was quiet. He had zero control. I knew he was suffering and to be totally honest I was delighting in it. I held my head high as I drove, chose the music, called the shots. This 6'1" man who used to be strong had wasted away into a skinny, stale-liquor-and-B.O.-smelling, cigarette-stained heap of flesh in my passenger seat.

When I dropped him off at rehab the main building was beautiful. I remember feeling resentful that he got to stay there and I had to go home—alone—to deal with the rent situation. What I did take note of were the women there. The offsite housing was separated by gender but I didn't know that yet. I was sure he'd cheat on me but I couldn't care less at that point. He had been doing that all along. It's why he accused me all the time.

Being home alone was eerie at first but it didn't take long for me to absolutely love it. I played my music, danced in the kitchen, cooked what I wanted, went where I wanted, and went to sleep when I wanted. I explained the situation to the landlord and he worked with me to get back on track with the rent. I went to work. I lived my life uninterrupted.

I was in control.

Until he got access to a phone.

The phone became my tether. I was trapped by a man who was in a cage. I followed his rules as if he were right next to me. Tame.

He would demand that I visit him as often as possible and sometimes he would sneak me in after hours. Sex was mandatory. To make sure I wasn't getting it anywhere else, he said, even though I was sure he was. I was going through the motions. This was just a series of habits played on repeat. There was no point but to satisfy his wants and needs.

By the time he came home we were able to have a conversation about the direction of our lives for the first time ever. We decided together that it wasn't the time to have a child and that FINALLY I should go on birth control. This was huge! I finally had a say over my reproductive rights. Before I called my OBGYN, I took a test to be sure we were in the clear.

I was pregnant. Again. For the third time.

Being pregnant was like every other day. I worked grooming dogs, managing a shop by myself. I was on my feet all day, with the same lifting, the same workload. I was not treated tenderly like I saw happen for other women. I wanted that. I wanted doors opened, bags carried, and baths drawn. I wanted ice cream and belly rubs. I wanted warm blankies and snuggles, to be told that my changing body was beautiful, to be held and cherished. That didn't happen. It was everyday life except I was getting fatter.

The people at church were so happy for us. We finally got our chance to have a baby, hoping this one would make it. They did, however, make it very clear that if we were to continue attending that church we had to get married before the baby was born. The people I grew to know as my family were giving us an ultimatum. Marriage or excommunication. And so a ring was bought from a guy on the street and unceremoniously given to me. We were engaged.

After losing two pregnancies I was terrified of another loss. I wasn't sure I could withstand that again. He only hit me on one occasion during the third pregnancy. I was home cooking dinner and he came bursting inside the door followed by a woman who was clearly a prostitute. Her hair was blonde with dark roots, scraggly and disheveled. She had makeup on but it was wearing off, mascara running down one cheek. Her face looked tired and afraid, obviously because she was running from something. She was wearing a black halter-top and a turquoise latex mini skirt. I could see part of her red thong peeking out the top of her skirt. She wasn't wearing stockings but was wearing black canvas sneakers and carrying a pair of high heels. Her purse was falling off her shoulder as she lumbered her tall skinny frame with pale bruised arms and legs through my home. I had never seen her before and I never saw her again after that.

There was no question, no explanation, just my terrorist fiancé followed by a strung out prostitute running through the home I was cooking dinner in, pregnant.

He ushered her in one end of the apartment and out the other. I wish I knew what my facial expression looked like. I was livid. Who was she? Why was he helping her? What the hell was going on? All he said was that she was running from the cops and he was helping her. My pregnant self could not stay calm. I went off screaming at him. "You put me in danger to help HER? Who the hell is she? What if the cops come here? Are you gonna pull this when the baby is born? Are you stupid?"

Smack.

My cheek was burning. I was shocked but I shouldn't have been. "Shut the fuck up you stupid bitch! That's none of your business!" It was my business. They were perfectly reasonable questions but I wasn't allowed to ask them. It turned into an argument, both of us screaming. When he came toward me, all I could think about was the baby. I positioned myself in the corner like someone being frisked, to brace myself and protect my stomach. I was hit from behind, mostly in the head. Ears ringing. Pain. Terror. And I know enough about my mindset back then to know that if I were to lose that pregnancy too, I'd have blamed myself for speaking up in the first place. I'd have blamed myself like he blamed me for the first two times, saying I wasn't strong enough to carry a child.

When it was over he left and I called the pastor of my church, a man I love and admire more than most people I know. He is always warm and caring. He reminds me of my own grandfather. I told him what had happened and he said to lock the door and call the cops. I locked the door but didn't call the cops. He said he didn't want to marry us and that he didn't believe I should stay. He offered to get me services if I decided to leave. I stayed inside and talked to him until the banging on the door began. The pastor told me not to open the door but eventually I did. All I heard from Scott were profuse apologies and tears. He needed help. He needed prayer. It wasn't him it was the devil inside of him. He promised things would be better once we were married. He promised things would be better when the baby was born. He promised it would never happen again. All lies that I chose to believe for no earthly reason at all. I convinced the pastor, after much pleading and many conversations, that things would be better. We had to go to church more and have faith-based accountability people assigned to us, but we complied and things proceeded toward the wedding.

Wedding planning was time-sensitive, as babies don't wait. To say that this event was haphazardly arranged would be a gross understatement. All decisions were made out of necessity or because it was a cheap option. My dress was bought at a department store at the mall because it was stretchy. The colors were black and red because, well, those were the colors of things people already had. My middle sister was kind enough to pay for the flowers. Red. My two sisters wore black dresses they already had, not matching in style but in color.

On the day of our wedding Scott had cold feet, apparently, although the only one who had anything to lose from this union was me. I walked down the aisle like a robot. Numb.

I remember my aunt being in the room where I was getting dressed, looking right into my eyes and offering to drive me away, wherever I wanted to go. Anywhere. I thought about it but declined. I had my blinders firmly on that day like a warhorse running through a minefield. Smile in place, eyes wide, blind.

The ceremony was short and sweet. We ate with our guests in the basement of the church, food prepared by my father and served by his friends. My mother, who was supposed to get our cake, asked me what I wanted. I told her red velvet. She brought a different kind so my dad had his friend make us a red velvet cake.

After the reception Gram told the pastor, "You have no idea what you've just done." She left, disgusted.

As my family and my church family began to disperse, we were told we could go celebrate. Not too much, though, as I was six months pregnant. We stopped at Wal-Mart on the way home from church to have our wedding pictures taken. Not a proud moment for me but it was all we could afford. He insisted we order a large canvas print of a close up shot of us. It was gaudy. I hated it. He loved it like any satisfied peacock would.

After our photo shoot we went back to our apartment, ordered Chinese food, and watched a Blockbuster movie. That's it. No honeymoon. Just us in the same place with another nail in my coffin.

The Casino

I stopped hoping for a happy husband, and simply hoped for one who wasn't my own private terrorist. Another argument. More of my things broken. Better than being hit this time, I suppose. Then again, is it? Per protocol, Scott confiscated my phone and keys after our spat. Now the driver of my car, he proceeded to stop at the liquor store.

Scott's friend Marlon was in the back seat with his girlfriend Shawnee. We weren't sure where we were going. Scott liked the control—the play for power was his favorite game so no one dared ask. Scott drove to an apartment building, a few blocks from ours, and pulled into the driveway. I knew this place. The canary yellow three-family house with green shutters and colored Christmas lights still up past the holidays was home to his cocaine dealer. At that point I knew enough to be nervous. *Here we go!* My hands became clammy and I remember my foot tapping much faster than the song on the radio.

Scott and Marlon went in and came back out. I know that Shawnee and I spoke to each other but I can't remember what we said. I assumed this was going to be just another night of him getting high at our house with his friend while I cleaned up their mess. I was wrong.

The guys came back out of the yellow apartment and sat in the car.

Scott pulled out the clear plastic bag from his pocket and then a Blockbuster card. He filled the corner with powder and inhaled quickly, twice each nostril. Then he did the same thing and held to the card to my face. I didn't want to get high. I don't like cocaine. The drip hurt my throat and made me feel like I wanted to crawl out of my skin.

"Do it. Stop being a little pussy!" he screamed, and motioned for his left pocket, one of his signature threats. I never found out what was in that pocket because I always did exactly as he said. It could have been a knife, a gun, or a picture of the Pope. The cocaine was passed around like the collection plate at church, and we were off.

As Scott drove, the music blared, some rap music and an occasional song that mentioned love, during which he would grab my hand and hold it affectionately, appearing to have no concept of what he was actually doing. I stayed quiet. Apparently Marlon wasn't in on the plan so he piped up, "Yo! Where the fuck we goin?"

Scott just laughed.

"The casino."

"Nah. Fuck that, man. I got shit to do."

Scott just laughed…and swerved my car like he was going to sideswipe into the one to our right.

"Oh shit!" Was the only other thing I heard from the backseat until we got there.

The casino was packed. The colors, sounds, and smells overwhelmed me. It felt like the Cirque du Soleil of desperation. "Would you like a drink?" asked a passing waitress. "Yes," I said as I took whatever she had on her tray.

I don't gamble. I'm not what I'd consider lucky. (Yes, I'm laughing as I write this.) We left after losing $500 in an hour. I was stunned at the amount of money he threw away. That could have helped me with our rent, our bills, and our groceries. At one point Marlon tried to convince Scott that he was too drunk, high, and angry to drive. We wanted to take a taxi home. Once again Scott motioned to his left pocket, and obediently into the car we went. They were my last hope of not getting into the car with him. But I couldn't say anything. It would have only made things worse.

Soon the pumping music became clouded by the driver's raspy cackle of a voice, "You stupid fucking bitch! I try to do fun things and you always ruin it! You don't ever appreciate shit," he shouted as he swerved in and out of lanes between cars and trucks. Shawnee screamed from the backseat as Marlon swore and threatened, both in fear for their lives.

And then there was me.

I sat in the passenger seat of my own car. No screaming, no pleading, no sudden movements. I knew that any attempt could result in death—one way or another. There was chaos and terror in the backseat, attempts at calming the situation, but I knew better than to try any of that. I wanted to turn around and tell them to shut up, but instead I closed them off as if there was a partition. I couldn't help them anymore. I couldn't help anyone.

I reached for my seatbelt and slowly drew it across my body, clicking it successfully into place. It was Scott and me now. The madman and the mouse.

He continued to rant and rave. His words had already cut me so deep that the scars invited them in. It was then that I looked out the window. The trees that lined the highway had turned into houses and backyards. Inside some of them I could see people. My mind invited me into those homes. A mom, dad, children, a dog, a meal on the table. They all looked so happy. Maybe they'll play a game after dinner, watch a TV show or read a book. Meatloaf, Candy Land, bedtime. Maybe they'll go outside and toss a ball around as the dog tries to catch it in an impressive feat of fur and skill. Maybe the mom is having a glass of wine as she pops a bag of popcorn and the dad gets a movie ready. What will they watch? *Shrek? Homeward Bound? E. T.?*

The faster he drove the slower the houses seemed to pass by, which brought me comfort. It gave me a chance to spend more time with the people inside. I was there with them, in their normal little homes, eating their normal little meals, petting their normal little dogs. They couldn't see me, but that was okay. I had become used to being invisible.

THE BIRTH

I WORKED FOR as long as I could while I was pregnant because I knew my income would be the last steady money I would see for a while. That's a terrifying thought with a baby on the way. I worked so far into my pregnancy that I had customers who refused to make their next grooming appointment with me, stating that they didn't want to see me working.

That's how little I cared for myself during that time. That's how little he cared for me during that time. Strangers were nicer to me than he was.

I had a bag packed weeks before my due date but I realized how unprepared I actually felt when the labor pains started in the middle of the night. Instantly, I felt my primal maternal instincts take over. I was terrified of the unknown, scared by how painful the contractions were, and excited to finally meet my baby. I didn't wake Scott up right away. I took that quiet time to make my final preparations. Around six a.m. he woke up. He knew immediately what was happening and called my middle sister. I had asked her to give us a ride (Scott had totaled my car) and to be in the room while I gave birth. My sister arrived quickly and the three of us headed to the hospital.

When we got there, the doctors immediately examined me. They determined I wasn't dilated enough to stay in the hospital so I was discharged and sent home to continue with my labor. I found it amusing when the doctor suggested I take a nap. How could anyone sleep when it felt like your insides were being squeezed like a wet kitchen sponge?

When I felt ready to go back to the hospital, I realized Scott had left. I was so deep in my own mind, trying to focus and breathe through the excruciating pain, that I don't know how long I had been left alone. My sister was at work, so I contacted his friend for a ride. He helped me down the stairs and into his car. It was just the two of us with no husband in sight. I started getting really angry and upset. I began to cry. We sat in the car and waited.

After 15 minutes, which felt like an eternity, Scott appeared. He jumped into the passenger seat and said *he* was ready. (I later found out that he was down the street, buying pot.)

My daughter was born at 11:22 p.m. weighing 7 pounds and 4 ounces and 19.5 inches long. I had given birth to a healthy baby girl! Scott was generally unhelpful during my labor and delivery. His focus was on going outside to smoke. It certainly wasn't on me.

But I did it. I remember holding my daughter for the first time and feeling something I have never felt before. Pure love. I was totally and completely responsible for this tiny person, this innocent little girl. I had always wished for someone to protect me when I was a little girl and I knew in that moment I couldn't let anything bad happen to her. I couldn't let her father grab hold of her.

For the first time I began to see clearly who and what he was because I had to for her. She changed everything for me. She gave me a reason to fight, to change my life, to stand up for myself, to heal and love myself for the first time ever. She gave me a reason to live.

There were so many times I was sure he was going to kill me and to be honest, I didn't care if I lived or died. But after I had my daughter all of that changed. If he did succeed in killing me, he would be her only parent. She would be at his mercy and my family would have to fight for custody.

There was the spark. There was the flame. There was the fire.

THE BREAK-IN

SHORTLY AFTER THE birth of my daughter I left Scott and we divorced. (That's a simple sentence for what wasn't simple at all.) I was living in the in-law apartment at my aunt and Gram's house. Things had been hard for so long that I couldn't sleep without pharmaceutical help. The expectation that I could just close my eyes and rest without seeing images from the past was too much. I couldn't do it. When I finally did drift off, I was like a corpse. I was so exhausted and stressed that once I closed my eyes, I was dead to the world.

I'd get my daughter to bed and then watch TV until my eyes felt like they might burn in their sockets. I'd get lost in watching the actors live their fake TV lives. It distracted me from mine. I wanted a fake TV life. I wanted to be happy like these people were pretending to be.

On this night I took my sleeping pill and followed it with beer. Was I drunk? I don't know. Possibly. If not, I was certainly headed in that direction. I don't know what time I fell asleep or remember what show I was watching when I did. All I know is that I made it to bed

I didn't hear the door. I didn't hear the dogs.

I woke up to Scott on top of me in my bed. At first I thought it was another nightmare. This man and his evening infiltrations, my nightmares his center stage. *Snap out of it, Sarah. It's just a dream.*

And then he leaned in so close his face was right in front of mine. I could smell the cheap brandy mixed with cigarettes—an all too familiar cologne. Once I realized it was real, my heart started pounding like it was going to fly out of my chest. I felt like I was going to throw up. He was straddled on top of me with each hand on one of my shoulders. He wasn't holding them down but he easily could have. "You don't say no to me," he whispered. It wasn't angry. There was no aggression in his voice. He said it as a matter of fact. He was right. Up until recently I hadn't said no to him. There was really no point. My "no" never really mattered.

By this time I was awake. My heart was racing and my adrenaline was pumping. "The baby's sleeping right in there," I seethed, and I motioned to her bedroom. The door to her room was about 10 feet from my bed. I was terrified he'd wake her up and she'd see us. She had no idea what he had done to me, the kind of pain he'd inflicted. She deserved her innocence.

"Then you better shut the fuck up," he said.

I could have screamed. My aunt was sleeping in the room at the top of the stairs. But my screams would have woken up my daughter. God forbid he hurt her physically, but the mental and emotional scars would have haunted her forever. I couldn't let that happen, so I stayed quiet.

He undressed me hastily, like someone pulling the burlap sack off of 50 pounds of potatoes. I distinctly remember my thighs jiggling a little as he took my pajama pants off. Then they started to shake on their own. I knew what he came for. At that point, though, what was the difference? He'd raped me so many times before that it had become routine. Fighting only made it worse, so I didn't. It was safer that way. It hurt less. As he took my shirt off, part of the sleeve ripped. Another thing ripped, broken, smashed, destroyed. He didn't care. Nothing about me mattered to him unless I was serving his needs. When he was done taking, he'd dismiss, disregard, and move on. I was a thing, a conquest. Even after our divorce he wanted to show me that I was still his. He came to take what he wanted and to remind me that I never really would be free of him.

Maybe that night he saw the defiance in my eyes. Maybe it was the blank stare that came after. I don't know. All I remember was his fist.

"Good morning, sunshine. Good morning, sunshine. Good morning, sunshine." My cell phone's alarm sang David Spade's voice, a scene from *Tommy Boy*. Groggily, I awoke, naked and with a pain in my head, wishing what had happened was just a dream.

I forced myself out of bed, pulled on the first clothes I could find, and went into my daughter's room to make sure she hadn't been harmed. My peaceful little girl. She was snuggled up in her blankets looking much like she usually did every morning. She sleeps like a bear. For that I will always be grateful.

Once I knew she was safe, I went about my morning. I let my dogs out, got my work clothes on, washed my face, brushed my teeth, did my hair and makeup, woke the sleeping bear, made our breakfasts, fed her, fed myself, let the dogs in, left to drop her off at daycare, drove to work and so on. The day was another day. This Novocain hovering across my existence was familiar. Autopilot switch was on.

I later realized that my gold chain, with the small oval medallion of Jesus, was missing. He had taken the chain off my neck while I was unconscious and was wearing it when he got arrested two days later. His probation officer had him arrested for noncompliance. My chain has remained in his property in prison, my stolen gold chain. When he gets out he will have it to wear. His trophy intact.

Why Didn't I Just Leave?

WHY DID SHE stay? Why didn't she just leave?

I used to wonder the same thing.

Why?

Love.

The love I had for him, anyway. My twisted self-sacrificing, masoch-istic version of it. I stayed because I became nostalgic for what I thought we were or could have been. That what I thought I saw in him was really there somewhere. That I hadn't wasted time trying to build a life with someone who hurt me. That my attempts to fix, help, and change this man were not futile. I was also embarrassed by what had happened to my life. I was ashamed to tell anyone the whole truth. I was in full denial of how bad the situation was. Even now the reality of what happened hits me in waves and I get emo-tional. I blamed myself for our failures, as I had been trained to do for so long. I gained a new perspective on love when a dear friend and colleague asked me, "What would you do if a stranger did, or said, any number of the things Scott did to you? Would you see them again? Would you invite them into your home? Would you give them an endless amount of second chances?" To which I answered emphatically, "No." That's when it became clear to me:

The blind love we have for our abusers is part of what keeps us in the cycle of abuse.

Money.

After having my daughter I stayed home with her. This was extremely difficult because I was accustomed to being the one with a stable job and steady income. Depending on him was so stressful, but I was a new mom with no job and no money. I didn't see my options. To be honest, I didn't think I had any. I have come to learn that there are generally two ways an abuser will use money as a means of controlling the victim. One is like what happened to me. I made the steady money, I paid the bills, I was the financially responsible one. I was used for the money I earned, plain and simple. I believed I was invest-ing in "us" when really he had no intention of reciprocating. This was coupled with the message that I wasn't good enough, that I was stupid, and that I was lucky he put up with me (blah blah blah). That was done in order to keep me, the breadwinner, always second-guessing myself; making me feel like I needed the one who, in reality, needed me. The other way money is used in abuse is to control all of the household funds. Some abusers require that their partner stay home in order to keep them dependent, while belittling them for not doing enough to contribute. Some let their partner work but take their check and manage the money, giving them an "allowance" that is controlled and monitored by the abuser. Whether using one for money or con-trolling all the funds, the victim is left with little to no money to escape if they need to. Now, in my studies of domestic violence, I've come to realize how crippling financial control can be to someone who is trying to leave an abusive relationship.

Defeat.

For a very long time I lost all hope of a better life. It was only after my daughter was born that I knew I had to do better for her. My daughter gave me the courage, strength, and motivation to leave. I had to live so I could be her mom. I couldn't let him kill me and be her only surviving parent. Some women stay in an abusive relationship because of their children. They don't want to break up their family. Almost always the abuser uses the children as a tool to manipulate the victim, saying they are a bad parent for considering leaving, that breaking up the family is their fault because it's their choice to take the kids and go. Not me. I knew I had to protect my daughter at all costs and give her the life she deserves. I refused to teach her that being abused is an acceptable way to be treated, because of my choice, my example as a woman.

Fear.

I was threatened, my pets were threatened, and so were my family members. I was told that he would find me no matter where I went and that he would hurt anyone who tried to help me. I believed him. I had no reason not to. It wasn't a matter of love; it was a matter of ownership and control. He used the people and all the things I love against me in order to keep me in the cycle of our dysfunctional relationship. He would abuse me and I would leave; he would threaten then apologize; and I would come back. Repeat. With the cycle of abuse it becomes a pattern, a habit, almost a dance. He played his part I played mine. We knew what to do and what to expect from each other. I lied for him. I made excuses for his behavior. I was trained to function under the tumultuous conditions of our relationship. I became used to the drama and dysfunction. It became comfortable for me to always be on high alert, hypervigilant, in defense mode. I learned my place in it.

Obligation.

I had spent so much time, energy, effort, and money investing in Scott. I thought I could save him from the path he was on and redirect his life to a better place. Once we were married I believed the vows I took. I made a commitment. The circumstances of that commitment were less than ideal, yes, but I planned on standing by my word. I thought if I worked harder, gave more, needed less, sacrificed, and did what he said, things would improve and we would be happy. These were all lies he told me and that I told myself. Over time I came to realize that it was never in my power, nor was it even my place, to "fix" him. What I thought was my obligation was really one of the many tethers that kept me stuck in the cycle of dysfunction.

Self-Worth.

This is so important and best taught young, if you ask me. My childhood was riddled with mixed messages, confusing events, trauma, attempts at creating order amid chaos, and taking care of those who were not my responsibility. It wasn't all bad, but the confusing combination of care and neglect left me trying to make sense of it all. I didn't understand how I deserved to be treated. There were no concrete examples for me. If you tell a child they can do anything they put their mind to then show them limited options with conditional support, chances are that child will grow up to believe, and mirror, what they saw and not what they heard. Self-worth is taught through a series of life lessons, examples of empowerment, and a balance between comfort and encouragement paired with structure, rules, and discipline. When the message is skewed, kids tend to blame themselves. Bringing up a child in an environment where they feel unsafe and there is little to no structure, makes them question their self-worth and believe that they deserve less than other kids. That's what I grew up to believe. For me the transition from home life to abuse was more seamless than some would like to believe. But that was, in fact, my experience.

How'd I Get Out?

I can't tell you the whole story of how I got out, for my own safety and for the safety of the people who were there for me. Besides, how I did it really isn't the point. The point is that anyone *can* leave an abusive relationship. People's safety/exit plan will be tailored to their specific circumstances. Everyone's case is different and must be assessed in such a way that puts safety above all else.

What I can share with you is that I was creating my safety/exit plan with a domestic violence (DV) counselor at the time Scott was arrested so I never had to carry it out.

And I can tell you what it takes to leave.

It takes brutal honesty. You need to be absolutely honest with yourself and the people around you. Telling the truth about your situation is the only way to get the help you need. I know that a huge part of the pattern of abuse is denial but I believe there is a part of us that knows that violence, manipulation, and pain are not love.

You have to be open to change and discomfort. Yes, we have been trained to find comfort in the absolutely terrifying day-to-day existence that is surviving domestic violence. Change is always hard. It's uncomfortable. It's frustrating, scary, emotional, and difficult. There are adjustments and sacrifices to be made. There is fear, but a different kind than the fear we're used to. We become afraid of the unknown: shelters, finances, schooling, threats, and our children's mental and emotional state. It's one of the reasons why so many victims continue to stay or go back after they've left. You have to be prepared to push through this period of time. I highly recommend you get a strong support system including a counselor and an accountability partner to process your feelings with as you move through this stage. It's crucial to have someone who is educated in the dynamics of domestic violence and can connect you with resources to help you through. I also recommend finding a DV support group. There is something unique and special about being in a room full of people who understand exactly what you're going through. Most people who haven't experienced it can't possibly understand all the dynamics of domestic violence—the challenges, emotions, pain, and struggles. A support group will help you realize that you are not alone, that you are not the only one who is going through this terrible experience, and that it's not your fault. It will give you the perspective you'll need to step outside the cycle and begin to make changes.

You need to be strong. I know you feel weak after what you've been through but I need you to look deep down inside yourself and find the motivation to pull yourself up from that low place. Maybe you feel so tired you can't even think straight. Most likely you have experienced gaslighting. Maybe you feel scared, terrified. Maybe you are so afraid to go outside, for fear that your abuser will be there or anywhere you go, for that matter. If that's the case, I urge you to talk to someone about it. Change your routine. Take a self-defense class to help you feel more powerful and in control. Maybe you feel angry, you want justice, you still feel enraged at what has happened to you—understandably so. But don't get trapped in anger. It has the ability to consume you. Instead, take that anger, that powerful emotion, and let it motivate you, drive you to make change. There is strength in letting go of what happened to you. By no longer allowing it to define your life you are stripping your abuser of their power.

Know that healing is a process. It takes time, energy, and effort.

Love yourself enough to do this work. It won't be easy. I know this to be true. Don't get frustrated with yourself. Cut yourself some slack.

But above all else, please forgive yourself for all the things you said and did; the lies you told; the ways you may have compromised your morals or sacrificed your integrity; or how you may have prioritized the wrong person/things.

You have to forgive yourself and move forward—for yourself, your friends, family, and children.

To someone who is trying to help someone leave:

Please be patient. Please be kind. Please research the dynamics of abuse and the effects that they have on the victim. By educating yourself and understanding what that person is most likely going through, you will be more equipped to help them. I urge you to contact your local domestic violence organization. Ask a counselor how to approach that person so you can better understand what they need, how to talk to them, and how to help. Victims are often terrified and they don't know who, or how, to trust. They've been brainwashed to believe that abuse is love and that outsiders make things worse. They are taught to keep it all a secret. They've been threatened, abused, and manipulated.

Please—don't judge them. This is the worst thing you could do. They have been judged, criticized, and belittled for far too long. Please pay attention to the words you use and the spirit in which you use them. If you are incapable of saying things kindly and without judgment, then find someone who can. Sometimes friends or family members are too close to the person. They can't separate themselves from the situation. If that is the case for you, do not take a front row seat in that person's recovery. They will need more love and support than you could possibly imagine. Please know that by being too harsh toward the victim, you run the risk of pushing them right back into the hands of their abuser. Nobody wants this outcome.

Here are a few examples of what not to say:

"If I were you I would/wouldn't…" Stop right there. It's not happening to you, it's happening to them. This isn't about you. It does not help the victim to know what you would or wouldn't do, or tolerate. The underlying unspoken message you're sending is that you are stronger and smarter than the victim, when in reality you have no idea what you would or wouldn't do if faced with their reality. Come from a place of compassion in an attempt at understanding and helping. It's better to say nothing than to say something harmful.

"To fix things you should try…" It's possible that there simply is no fixing things. It's possible there is no change other than to separate and cut ties. Also, the person you're speaking with has most likely tried a plethora of ways to "fix" the situation. If an abuser is set on keeping the victim in the cycle of abuse there will be no fix.

"Why didn't/did you…?" Look, if someone is telling you a story of what they've been through, you should feel privileged that they're even talking to you about it. They're most likely desperate for someone to reach out to. They want to be heard and understood. Looking back at what someone could have or should have done, in your opinion, does not help anyone.

"What did you do to make at happen?" You might think we're past the times of this question being asked but we're most certainly not. People have asked me that very thing. I cannot stress this enough. If you wonder that in your mind as someone is telling you about being abused, then part of the problem lies within you. Do not let those words leave your mouth. I'm asking you to stop and ask yourself why you would blame the victim for being abused. I encourage you to question what makes you think that way? Foster compassion and understanding rather than judgment and condemnation.

Here are a few examples of what to say:

"How can I help you? What do you need?" Every abuse victim/survivor is different and so are their needs. By asking that person how you can help, you are sending the message that you care and you are giving them a piece of the control they've been robbed of. It's as simple as that. Stay engaged. Listen to what they are saying and try to listen for what they are not saying. I have found that many breakthroughs lie in what is unsaid.

"It's not your fault. You don't deserve to be treated that way." People who are abused have been blamed by their abuser for things that couldn't possibly be their fault. It changes the way they think about themselves and the people around them. They begin to accept the blame and learn to blame themselves. The shift is always focused on them: how they messed up, how they have to fix it. They will apologize often, for things that do not require an apology. By reminding them that things are not their fault and telling them that they deserve better, you could begin to open their eyes to reality.

"I'm here for you." If you say this, make sure you're ready to follow through. When making life decisions, abuse victims/survivors need a strong support system. They need to know who will and won't be there when things become more difficult. There is nothing worse than being disappointed by someone you need when you're right in the thick of needing them.

"What could you do next time?" This is the beginning of creating a plan. By asking this question you are inserting the notion that things can be different. You are empowering the victim to think in the direction of changing their pre-programmed response. There is no judgment in this question. It is direct, straightforward. Creating a plan is one of the keys to taking back one's power and beginning to create change in their own life.

"I don't have the answers but I'll help you find someone who does." If you have no idea what to say or do, don't make it up as you go. There are systems in place for this very situation. When a person is leaving their abuser it is statistically one of the most dangerous times for them. Things change in seconds. Danger increases. The abusive behavior escalates. Do yourself and the victim a favor. Let them know you will not leave them alone in this but that there is someone who knows better than you. Also, please note that helpers can be put in harms way. Referring someone to professional help in the leaving process will keep them and you as safe as possible.

Finally, I encourage you to seek help for yourself as well. Supportive people need supportive people of their own. The circle of influence is deep and wide. Make sure to take care of yourself and your emotional stability so that you can be the most supportive person possible. Healing is a process that takes time and effort. It doesn't happen by accident and it doesn't come with a timeline. It is a beautiful process.

HOW'D YOU DO?

Hi.

How'd you do? I tried to make this book as palatable as possible, while still being true to the story. I hope you don't feel overwhelmed. If you do feel triggered by this, I urge you to talk to someone about it: a friend, family member, pastor, counselor, or colleague. Talking about this topic is another way you can help bridge the gap for those suffering and who still don't know anything about domestic violence. This book was written entirely with the intention to help and educate. I want to open people's eyes and create connections so that maybe we can save more lives together.

You read all the way through. You stuck with me. You've heard my story.

But this isn't really the end, is it?

It's more like a beautiful beginning as we begin to bring understanding, compassion, and connection to victims of domestic violence—what wonderful outcomes from a terrible situation!

To be honest with you, writing this book took me to a place that I never thought I'd return to. After practically a lifetime of disassociation, I chose to feel emotions in real time, possibly for the first time since I was a little girl, as I began to write this book. That's when my true healing began. It wasn't easy. I avoided writing and then got down on myself for not writing enough. I almost went so far as to check myself into a psych ward as I worked to complete my first draft. And that's the truth.

I'm not ashamed to share this with you and here's why: I am human. You are human. I have struggled through life and so have you. Maybe our struggles have been different, maybe they've been the same, but regardless, we are all connected through this human experience. I'm sure many people have had such extreme pain and sadness that they weren't sure how much longer they could take it. I know I have! But what I want you to know is that you can make a difference, despite your adversities. We all can, in our own way. I have by writing this book and you have by reading this book. Every word counts, because they're all part of something bigger, just like us.

If you think there's nothing you can do to help make a difference to those who are suffering through abuse, please reconsider. You can donate your time, talent, and funds. You can educate yourself and others. You can reach out to a friend or ask a stranger if they need help. If you want to know more, get involved with your local DV shelter or with an advocacy group. Keep up with the laws that affect domestic violence victims, survivors, and their families. If you are someone who needs help, please be brave and be honest. First and foremost, be honest with yourself. You deserve a life of happiness and safety, not one of pain and suffering.

Thank you again for reading this book. It was hard to write, and at times I didn't want to do it. But here we are! Please spread love and awareness. Please be a little more compassionate and understanding to all people. You never know what the person in front of you has been through. It could very well be a story like mine.

Love, Light & Blessings Always,
~Sarah Gallardo
Founder and Executive Director, Sarah Speaks Up
SarahSpeaksUp.org

If you or someone you know needs help, please call the National Domestic Violence Hotline at 1-800-799-SAFE.

Sarah Speaks Up

AFTER THE BIRTH of my daughter I started attending a weekly domestic violence support group. I began to learn about red flags, the dynamics of power and control, narcissistic behavior, and what love actually looked and felt like.

I was so comforted by the fact that I wasn't alone. There were others like me who understood what I was going through because they had gone through it themselves. We helped each other through whatever we were experiencing at the time. We shared stories. We laughed, cried, and held each other together as best we could.

After four years of one-on-one and group therapy, I became a certified domestic violence counselor as a result of the nudging of our group counselor, a dear friend and colleague. I began giving speeches and interviews, writing poetry about my experience and reciting it at events. I became involved in fund-raising for the cause, always working hard to support local organizations and spread awareness so as to help as many people as I could. I realized that there could never be enough funds and awareness for domestic violence. I decided to step out of the shadows and form Sarah Speaks Up, a nonprofit organization that works to support victims and survivors of domestic violence.

One of the most beautiful outcomes of the advocacy work I do now is the people I meet. I met a wonderful man while sharing the story, "The Falling," at an event. There were sparks of connection between us. This man, who I would never have met if not for speaking up, turned out to be the love of my life, my partner, my person. He had already heard the worst of it all and yet he was still interested in me.

My daughter loves him and he loves her. She is flourishing under the light of the love we have for one another. We have begun to share in the responsibility of parenting her. We are cohesive. We have grown together in unexpected ways. THIS is what I signed up for. THIS is what I believe is worth sacrificing for. And the most beautiful thing of all is that we work together. We communicate fairly, we learn about each other's likes and dislikes, wants and needs. We prioritize the other person, bending when necessary, apologizing sincerely when we've hurt the other person. I support him, he supports me, and we support her. We learn and grow right along with her, as a team.

I hope this kind of love for you.

I hope you can see the difference between what was and what is. I know I can feel the difference every day. Maybe the suffering I experienced in life was what needed to happen in order to make a difference.

Maybe the difference is him.

Maybe the difference is her.

Who knows, maybe it's me.

Maybe the difference is you.

SarahSpeaksUp.org

INVISIBLE

We are the beaten and bruised among you.

We are the ones who suffer in silence, covering cuts and scrapes with long sleeves, black eyes with makeup and split lips with excuses.

We are the ones who are controlled with a phone call, text or glance, clearing of the throat or tone of voice.

We are family members, friends, coworkers, strangers on the sidewalk who pass by you every single day.

There is no race, religion, demographic, financial status, and educational background, sexual orientation or even gender that defines us.

We see you every single day and you see us too but you don't know it.

Fear and embarrassment keep us quiet, our belief that we are, in fact, alone, and that you wouldn't believe the truth if you heard it.

Our reasons vary but still we are here parenting, paying bills or not, going to church, sporting events, work, the store, living our lives as best we can for as long as we can.

We hide in plain sight.

~ Sarah Gallardo

Resources

If you, are someone you love, is being abused, I encourage you to read the following information.

Please remember help is a phone call away: 1-800-799-SAFE

What Is Domestic Violence?

Domestic violence (also called intimate partner violence (IPV), domestic abuse, or relationship abuse) is a pattern of behaviors used by one partner to maintain power and control over another partner in an intimate relationship.

Domestic violence does not discriminate. Anyone of any race, age, sexual orientation, religion or gender can be a victim—or perpetrator—of domestic violence. It can happen to people who are married, living together, or who are dating. It affects people of all socioeconomic backgrounds and education levels.

Domestic violence includes behaviors that physically harm, arouse fear, prevent a partner from doing what they wish to or forcing them to behave in ways they do not want. It includes the use of physical and sexual violence, threats and intimidation, emotional abuse, and economic deprivation. Many of these different forms of domestic violence/abuse can be occurring at any one time within the same intimate relationship.

What are the Warning Signs?

It's not always easy to tell at the beginning of a relationship if it will become abusive.

In fact, many abusive partners may seem absolutely perfect in the early stages of a relationship. Possessive and controlling behaviors don't always appear overnight, but rather emerge and intensify as the relationship grows.

Domestic violence doesn't look the same in every relationship because every relationship is different. But one thing most abusive relationships have in common is that the abusive partner does many different kinds of things to have more power and control over their partner.

Some of the signs of an abusive relationship include a partner who:

- Tells you that you can never do anything right
- Shows extreme jealousy of your friends and time spent away
- Keeps you or discourages you from seeing friends or family members
- Insults, demeans, or shames you with put-downs
- Controls every penny spent in the household
- Takes your money or refuses to give you money for necessary expenses
- Looks at you or acts in ways that scare you
- Controls who you see, where you go, or what you do
- Prevents you from making your own decisions
- Tells you that you are a bad parent or threatens to harm or take away your children
- Prevents you from working or attending school
- Destroys your property or threatens to hurt or kill your pets
- Intimidates you with guns, knives, or other weapons
- Pressures you to have sex when you don't want to or does things sexually you're not comfortable with
- Pressures you to use drugs or alcohol

If you or someone you know needs help, please call the National Domestic Violence Hotline at 1-800-799-SAFE.

You may be experiencing physical abuse if your partner has done or repeatedly does any of the following tactics of abuse:

- Pulling your hair, punching, slapping, kicking, biting, or choking you
- Forbidding you from eating or sleeping
- Hurting you with weapons
- Preventing you from calling the police or seeking medical attention
- Harming your children
- Abandoning you in unfamiliar places
- Driving recklessly or dangerously when you are in the car with them
- Forcing you to use drugs or alcohol (especially if you've had a substance abuse problem in the past)

Source: http://www.thehotline.org/is-this-abuse/abuse-defined/

REPRODUCTIVE ABUSE

The most common question I get when I tell my story is, "What is reproductive abuse?"

Reproductive and sexual coercion involves behavior intended to maintain power and control in a relationship related to reproductive health by someone who is, was, or wishes to be involved in an intimate or dating relationship with an adult or adolescent.

Reproductive coercion is related to behavior that interferes with contraception use and pregnancy. The most common forms of reproductive coercion include sabotage of contraceptive methods, pregnancy coercion, and pregnancy pressure.

Birth control sabotage is active interference with a partner's contraceptive methods in an attempt to promote pregnancy. Examples include hiding, withholding, or destroying a partner's oral contraceptives; breaking or poking holes in a condom on purpose or removing a condom during sex in an attempt to promote pregnancy; not withdrawing when that was the agreed upon method of contraception; and removing vaginal rings, contraceptive patches, or intrauterine devices (IUDs).

Pregnancy pressure involves behavior intended to pressure a female partner to become pregnant when she does not wish to become pregnant. Pregnancy coercion involves coercive behavior such as threats or acts of violence if a partner does not comply with the perpetrator's wishes regarding the decision to terminate or continue a pregnancy. Examples of pregnancy pressure and coercion include threatening to hurt a partner who does not agree to become pregnant, forcing a partner to carry a pregnancy to term against her wishes through threats or acts of violence, forcing a female partner to terminate a pregnancy when she does not want to, or injuring a female partner in a way that may cause a miscarriage. Homicide is a leading cause of pregnancy-associated mortality in the United States. In one study, the majority of pregnancy-associated homicides were committed by an intimate partner.

Sexual coercion includes a range of behavior that a partner may use related to sexual decision making to pressure or coerce a person to have sex without using physical force. This behavior includes repeatedly pressuring a partner to have sex, threatening to end a relationship if the person does not have sex, forcing sex without a condom or not allowing other prophylaxis use, intentionally exposing a partner to a sexually transmitted infection (STI) including human immunodeficiency virus (HIV), or threatening retaliation if notified of a positive STI test result.

One quarter of adolescent females reported that their abusive male partners were trying to get them pregnant through interference with planned contraception, forcing the female partners to hide their contraceptive methods. In one study of family planning clinic patients, 15 percent of women experiencing physical violence also reported birth control sabotage. Among adolescent mothers on public assistance who experienced recent intimate partner violence (IPV), 66 percent experienced birth control sabotage by a dating partner. Compared with women not experiencing abuse, women experiencing physical abuse and women disclosing psychological abuse by an intimate partner had an increased risk of developing an STI.

Based on this information, health care providers should include reproductive and sexual coercion and IPV as part of the differential diagnosis when patients are seen for pregnancy testing or STI testing, emergency contraception, or with unplanned pregnancies. Intervention is critical.

Source: https://www.acog.org/Resources-And-Publications/Committee-Opinions/Committee-on-Health-Care-for-Underserved-Women/Reproductive-and-Sexual-Coercion

Financial Abuse

Financial abuse is a common tactic used by abusers to gain power and control in a relationship. The forms of financial abuse may be subtle or overt but in general, they include tactics to limit the partner's access to assets or conceal information and accessibility to the family finances. Financial abuse, along with emotional, physical, and sexual abuse, manipulation, intimidation, and threats are all intentional tactics used by an abuser aimed at entrapping the partner in the relationship. In some abusive relationships, financial abuse is present throughout the relationship and in other cases financial abuse becomes present when the survivor is attempting to leave or has left the relationship.

Financial abuse, while less commonly understood, is one of the most powerful methods of keeping a survivor trapped in an abusive relationship and deeply diminishes their ability to stay safe after leaving an abusive relationship. Research indicates that financial abuse is experienced in 98 percent of abusive relationships and surveys of survivors reflect that concern over their ability to provide financially for themselves and their children was one of the top reason for staying in or returning to a battering relationship. As with all forms of abuse, financial abuse occurs across all socio-economic, educational and racial and ethnic groups.

Forms of Financial Abuse

As with other forms of abuse, financial abuse may begin subtly and progress over time. It may even look like love initially as abusers have the capacity to appear very charming and are masterful at manipulation. For example, the abuser may make statements such as, "I know you're under a lot of stress right now so why don't you just let me take care of the finances and I'll give you money each week to take care of what you need." Under these circumstances, the victim may believe that they should or can trust the partner they are in love with and may willingly give over control of the money and how it is spent. This scenario commonly leads to the batterer giving the victim less and less in "allowance." By the time the victim decides they want to take back control of the finances, they discover that the accounts have all been moved or they no longer have knowledge or access to the family funds.

In other cases, the financial abuse may be much more overt. Batterers commonly use violence or threats of violence and intimidation to keep the victim from working or having access to the family funds. Whether subtle or overt, there are common methods that batterers use to gain financial control over their partner.

These include:

- Forbidding the victim to work
- Sabotaging work or employment opportunities by stalking or harassing the victim at the workplace or causing the victim to lose their job by physically battering prior to important meetings or interviews
- Controlling how all of the money is spent
- Not allowing the victim access to bank accounts
- Withholding money or giving an "allowance"
- Not including the victim in investment or banking decisions

- Forbidding the victim from attending job training or advancement opportunities
- Forcing the victim to write bad checks or file fraudulent tax returns
- Running up large amounts of debt on joint accounts or taking bad credit loans
- Refusing to work or contribute to the family income
- Withholding funds for the victim or children to obtain basic needs such as food and medicine
- Hiding assets
- Stealing the victim's identity, property, or inheritance
- Forcing the victim to work in a family business without pay
- Refusing to pay bills and ruining the victim's credit score
- Forcing the victim to turn over public benefits or threatening to turn the victim in for "cheating or misusing benefits"
- Filing false insurance claims
- Refusing to pay or evading child support or manipulating the divorce process by drawing it out by hiding or not disclosing assets

The Impact of Financial Abuse

The short- and long-term effects of financial abuse can be devastating. In the short term, access to assets is imperative to staying safe. Without assets, survivors are often unable to obtain safe and affordable housing or the funds to provide for themselves or their children. With realistic fears of homelessness, it is little wonder that survivors sometimes return to the battering relationship.

For those who manage to escape the abuse and survive initially, they often face overwhelming odds in obtaining long-term security and safety. Ruined credit scores, sporadic employment histories, and legal issues caused by the battering make it extremely difficult to gain independence, safety and long-term security.

Source: http://nnedv.org/resources/ejresources/about-financial-abuse.html

Unspoken Threats, Verbal Abuse

EMOTIONAL OR PSYCHOLOGICAL abuse is in a somewhat different category from verbal because an abuser can threaten, demean, or manipulate their victim without ever saying a word. For example, if the aim is to elicit fear and compliance, an abuser may throw their target a terrifying glare, ball up their fists, or make the shape of a gun with their fingers. In a combination of verbal and nonverbal tactics, words can be carefully chosen to produce manipulative results.

An abuser may frequently lie to or about his victim, play on their personal fears and tragedies, publicly embarrass them, or intentionally create conflicts within their personal and professional relationships. The victim's mental chaos aids and enables the abuser, so the abuser will often try to make the victim question their own sanity by engaging in psychological gameplay called "crazy-making" or "gaslighting." In the steps of this twisted dance, the abuser may hide the victim's car keys, disable their alarm clock, or steal their money, so they can later accuse them of being confused, forgetful, and irresponsible. This helps the abuser to then deny or minimize future abusive incidents by saying things like, "You're crazy. I never said or did that. It never happened."

It may be easier to understand why an abuser would adopt this behavior when we examine the benefits that it offers them. Verbal and mental abuse serves the following three important purposes for an abuser:

1. To decimate the victim's self-esteem so they are less likely to think they could leave, make it on their own, or find someone new. After years of hearing that they are worthless, ugly, stupid, or unlovable, the victim starts to believe it themselves. Then, they are dependent upon the abuser for emotional validation, thus insuring that they will stay weakened and firmly in place.

2. To shift the blame by convincing the victim that she is deeply flawed, and therefore responsible for the abuse. The victim will then attempt (in vain) to change themselves so they can "fix the problem," not realizing that it is the abuser who is at fault, and the victim can never live up to the unrealistic expectations which have been laid at their feet.

3. To make an "externally narcissistic/internally fragile" individual feel powerful and superior. Using verbal domination helps an abuser to control any interpersonal situation and avoid being questioned or held accountable for their actions. The victim remains in a constantly oppressed, "walking on eggshells" state, and if they dare to demonstrate any resistance, the abuser can always rely on the unspoken, overarching threat of physical and/or sexual violence.

Despite the lack of bruises and blood, verbal and psychological assaults are just as lasting and damaging as physical abuse because they send the victim crippling messages about their own power and value as a human being. In order to leave an unhealthy relationship, victims require outside support, economic resources, and self-confidence. By criticizing their intelligence, judgment, appearance, or capabilities, the abuser "clips their wings" and keeps them in danger. People who are the recipients of constant name-calling, insults, threats, and intimidation should be recognized as victims of domestic violence, and receive just as much attention, concern, and assistance as those who are physically assaulted.

Source: https://sealpress.com/2015/01/
sticks-and-stones-why-emotional-and-verbal-abuse-can-be-just-as-damaging-as-physical-abuse/

Gaslighting

Gaslighting is a tactic in which a person or entity, in order to gain more power, makes a victim question their reality.

It works much better than you may think.

Anyone is susceptible to gaslighting, and it is a common technique of abusers, dictators, narcissists, and cult leaders. It is done slowly, so the victim doesn't realize how much they've been brainwashed.

For example, in the movie Gaslight (1944), a man manipulates his wife to the point where she thinks she is losing her mind.

People who gaslight typically use the following techniques:

1. **They tell blatant lies.**

    You know it's an outright lie. Yet they are telling you this lie with a straight face. Why are they so blatant? Because they're setting up a precedent. Once they tell you a huge lie, you're not sure if anything they say is true. Keeping you unsteady and off-kilter is the goal.

2. **They deny they ever said something, even though you have proof.**

    You know they said they would do something; you know you heard it. But they out and out deny it. It makes you start questioning your reality—maybe they never said that thing. And the more they do this, the more you question your reality and start accepting theirs.

3. **They use what is near and dear to you as ammunition.**

   They know how important your kids are to you, and they know how important your identity is to you. So those may be one of the first things they attack. If you have kids, they tell you that you should not have had those children. They will tell you'd be a worthy person if only you didn't have a long list of negative traits. They attack the foundation of your being.

4. **They wear you down over time.**

   This is one of the insidious things about gaslighting—it is done gradually, over time. A lie here, a lie there, a snide comment every so often...and then it starts ramping up. Even the brightest, most self-aware people can be sucked into gaslighting—it is that effective. It's the "frog in the frying pan" analogy: The heat is turned up slowly, so the frog never realizes what's happening to it.

5. **Their actions do not match their words.**

   When dealing with a person or entity that gaslights, look at what they are doing rather than what they are saying. What they are saying means nothing; it is just talk. What they are doing is the issue.

6. **They throw in positive reinforcement to confuse you.**

   This person or entity that is cutting you down, telling you that you don't have value, is now praising you for something you did. This adds an additional sense of uneasiness. You think, "Well maybe they aren't so bad." Yes, they are. This is a calculated attempt to keep you off-kilter—and again, to question your reality. Also look at what you were praised for; it is probably something that served the gaslighter.

7. **They know confusion weakens people.**

   Gaslighters know that people like having a sense of stability and normalcy. Their goal is to uproot this and make you constantly question everything. And humans' natural tendency is to look to the person or entity that will help you feel more stable—and that happens to be the gaslighter.

8. **They project.**

They are a drug user or a cheater, yet they are constantly accusing you of that. This is done so often that you start trying to defend yourself, and are distracted from the gaslighter's own behavior.

9. **They try to align people against you.**

Gaslighters are masters at manipulating and finding the people they know will stand by them no matter what—and they use these people against you. They will make comments such as, "This person knows that you're not right," or "This person knows you're useless too." Keep in mind it does not mean that these people actually said these things. A gaslighter is a constant liar. When the gaslighter uses this tactic it makes you feel like you don't know who to trust or turn to—and that leads you right back to the gaslighter. And that's exactly what they want: Isolation gives them more control.

10. **They tell you or others that you are crazy.**

This is one of the most effective tools of the gaslighter, because it's dismissive. The gaslighter knows if they question your sanity, people will not believe you when you tell them the gaslighter is abusive or out-of-control. It's a master technique.

11. **They tell you everyone else is a liar.**

By telling you that everyone else (your family, the media) is a liar, it again makes you question your reality. You've never known someone with the audacity to do this, so they must be telling the truth, right? No. It's a manipulation technique. It makes people turn to the gaslighter for the "correct" information—which isn't correct information at all.

The more you are aware of these techniques, the quicker you can identify them and avoid falling into the gaslighter's trap.

Source: https://www.psychologytoday.com/blog/here-there-and-everywhere/201701/11-signs-gaslighting-in-relationship

WHY VICTIMS STAY

THE MOST FREQUENTLY asked question concerning a battering situation is why does the victim stay?

While there exists a variety of reasons, it is also very possible the victim may be locked into a cycle of violence.

Below are some of the most common reasons why victims stay with the batterers.

- The victim loves the batterer… the batterer is not always violent.
- The victim fears the batterer, believing the batterer to be almost "godlike." Often threats are made against the victim, for example, the batterer will kill the victim if the beatings are reported to anyone. Police, in the victim's eyes, offer no long-term protection from the batterer.
- Even if it is a neighbor who reports, the batterer may take it out on the victim. Often when the police come, the victim will not admit the battering.
- The victim may be economically dependent on the batterer and, not having a marketable job skill, the victim has no realistic alternative to the batterer's financial support.
- Socialization creates a powerful inertia in relationships, people feel they must stay in a relationship and are highly resistant to change as a means of problem solving.

- Socialization and/or religious or cultural beliefs demand that the victim maintain the facade of a good marriage.
- Often the batterer is the victim's only psychological support system, having systematically destroyed the victim's other friendships. Other people also feel uncomfortable around violence and withdraw from it.
- Learned helplessness. The victim has been taught and believes to be powerless, and therefore views the situation from that perspective.
- Often the victim stays for the sake of the children "needing a father," or the batterer may make threats of violence against the children if the victim tries to leave. The batterer frequently threatens to take the children away from the victim if the victim leaves, and the victim believes the batterer.
- The victim believes law enforcement and judicial authorities in some jurisdictions may not take domestic violence seriously, hence the victim believes the batterer is often not punished or removed from the victim. Yet any attempts by the victim to consult authorities are seen as a threat by the batterer and he/she may beat the victim for that.
- Sometimes the batterer is otherwise well respected or mild mannered, so the victim's concerns are not taken seriously. Often the batterer is violent only with the victim and frequently concludes there is something wrong with the victim.
- The victim may rationalize the beatings, believing that the victim must have "deserved" the "punishment" or that the batterer was just "too drunk" to know what the batterer was doing (beliefs the batterer propagates).
- The victim may have no idea that services are available and may feel trapped.
- The battering takes place during a relatively short period of time. Afterwards the batterer may be quite gentle,

apologetic, loving, and may promise never to beat the victim again.

- The victim may be convinced that this beating will be the last.
- The victim may have lived in a home in which one parent beat the other and/or the children and sees violence as an inevitable part of the way in which couples relate.
- Often a battered person, motivated by pity and compassion, is convinced that the victim alone can help the batterer with the "problem" (whether it is drinking, "pressure from the outside world", "victim's mistakes", etc).
- Situational Factors

Economic dependence

- Fear of greater physical danger to self and children if they attempt to leave
- Fear of emotional damage to the children
- Fear of losing custody of the children
- Lack of alternative housing
- Lack of jobs skills
- Social isolation resulting in lack of support from family or friends and lack of information regarding alternatives
- Fear of involvement in court processes
- Cultural and religious constraints
- Fear of retaliation

Emotional Factors

- Fear of loneliness
- Insecurity over potential independence and lack of emotional support
- Guilt about failure of marriage
- Fear that partner is not able to survive alone

- Belief that partner will change
- Ambivalence and fear over making formidable life changes

The Stockholm or "Hostage" Syndrome

Many women feel locked into a "hostage" syndrome and thus continue to remain in an abusive relationship.

The victim of domestic violence:

- And the abuser are bidirectionally bonded
- Is intensely grateful for small kindnesses shown by the abuser
- Denies the abuser's violence against them, or rationalizes that violence
- Denies their own anger at the abuser
- Is hyper-vigilant to the abuser's needs and seeks to keep the abuser happy. To do this, the survivor tries to "get inside the abuser's head"
- Sees the world from the abuser's perspective, they may not have their own perspective
- Sees outside authorities trying to win their release (for example, police, parents) as "bad guys" and the abuser as the "good guy."
- Sees the abuser as the protector
- Finds it difficult to leave the abuser even after their release
- Fears the abuser will come back to get them even after the abuser is dead or in prison
- Shows symptoms of Post-Traumatic Stress Disorder (PTSD)
- Has a recurrent emotional reaction to a terrifying, uncontrollable, or life-threatening event
- Develops symptoms such as nightmares, overwhelming feelings of fear and anxiety, difficulty concentrating, and increased stress in relationships after a person's sense of safety and security are violated

- Symptoms and reactions are common and an important part of initial adjustment and later recovery.
- Some batterers are life endangering. It is possible to evaluate whether a batterer is likely
- to kill his partner, other family members, and/or others attempting intervention.
- The following are indicators often used in making an assessment of a batterer's potential to kill.
- Fantasies of Homicide or Suicide - The more the batterer has developed a fantasy about who, how, when and/or where to kill, the more dangerous the batterer may be. The batterer who has previously acted out part of a homicide or suicide fantasy may be invested in killing as a viable "solution" to the abuser's problem.
- Weapons - Where a batterer possesses weapons and has used them or has threatened to use them in the past assaults on the battered victim, the children, or self, the batterer's access to those weapons increases the potential for lethal assault.
- Obsessiveness about Partner or Family - A batterer who is obsessive about their partner, who either idolizes and feels that they cannot live without their partner, or believes they are entitled to their partner no matter what because they are their spouse, is more likely to be life-endangering.
- Centrality of the Battered Woman - If the loss of the battered victim represents or precipitates a total loss of hope for a positive future, a batterer may choose to kill.
- Rage - The most life endangering rage often erupts when a batterer believes the battered victim is leaving.
- Threats of Homicide or Suicide - The batterer who has threatened to kill himself/herself, his partner, the children, or her relatives must be considered extremely dangerous.
- Depression - Where a batterer has been acutely depressed

and sees little hope for moving beyond the depression, may be a candidate for homicide and suicide.

- Drug or Alcohol Consumption - Consumption of drugs or alcohol when in a state of despair or fury can elevate the risk of lethality.
- Pet Abuse - Those batterers who assault and mutilate pets are more likely to kill or maim family members.
- Access to the Battered Victim and/or Family Member - If the batterer cannot find the victim, the batterer cannot kill the victim.

Source: http://www.lapdonline.org/get_informed/ content_basic_view/8877

DISASSOCIATION

THIS IS THE act of disuniting or separating complex and unbearable emotions, experiences, and memories into parts. Separating usually connected mental processes (such as emotion and understanding) from the rest of the mind, as a defense mechanism, is a normal response to trauma, to varying degrees. In some cases, sustained trauma and abuse in early childhood results in dissociative identity disorder (formerly called multiple personality disorder).

The role of dissociation as the most direct defense against overwhelming traumatic experience was first documented in the seminal work of Pierre Janet. Recent research evaluating the relationship between Post-traumatic Stress Disorder (PTSD) and dissociation has suggested that there is a dissociative subtype of PTSD, defined primarily by symptoms of derealization (i.e., feeling as if the world is not real) and depersonalization (i.e., when a person feels as if he or she is not real).

In psychology, dissociation is any of a wide array of experiences from mild detachment from immediate surroundings to more severe detachment from physical and emotional experience. The major characteristic of all dissociative phenomena involves a detachment from reality, rather than a loss of reality as in psychosis.

Dissociation is commonly displayed on a continuum. In mild cases, dissociation can be regarded as a coping mechanism or defense mechanisms in seeking to master, minimize, or tolerate stress—including boredom or conflict.

At the nonpathological end of the continuum, dissociation describes common events such as daydreaming while driving a vehicle. Farther along the continuum are non-pathological altered states of consciousness.

More pathological dissociation involves dissociative disorders, including dissociative fugue and depersonalization disorder with or without alterations in personal identity or sense of self. These alterations can include: a sense that self or the world is unreal (depersonalization and derealization); a loss of memory (amnesia); forgetting identity or assuming a new self (fugue); and fragmentation of identity or self into separate streams of consciousness (dissociative identity disorder, formerly termed multiple personality disorder) and complex post-traumatic stress disorder.

Dissociative disorders are sometimes triggered by trauma, but may be preceded only by stress, psychoactive substances, or no identifiable trigger at all. The ICD-10 (*The International Classifications of Diseases*) classifies conversion disorder as a dissociative disorder. The *Diagnostic and Statistical Manual of Mental Disorders, 5*th *Edition* groups all dissociative disorders into a single category.

Although some dissociative disruptions involve amnesia, other dissociative events do not. Dissociative disorders are typically experienced as startling, autonomous intrusions into the person's usual ways of responding or functioning. Due to their unexpected and largely inexplicable nature, they tend to be quite unsettling.

Sources: https://en.wikipedia.org/wiki/Dissociation_(psychology)
http://snohomishcounseling.com/specialities/
domestic-violence-trauma-and-dissociation/

Use of Weapons in Domestic Violence

IN THE UNITED States, domestic violence claims at least 2,000 lives each year. Seventy percent of the victims are women. More than half of the time, the weapon used to carry out an "intimate partner" homicide—when a person targets a spouse, boyfriend or girlfriend, or someone with whom they previously had a romantic relationship—is a gun.

The link between guns and fatal domestic abuse is so strong, research shows that simply living in a state with a high rate of firearm ownership increases a woman's risk of being fatally shot in a domestic violence incident.

While the stats show that guns are used to kill women in 53 percent of intimate partner homicides, they are responsible for 70 percent of these collateral victims. Of police officers slain while responding to domestic disputes, 95 percent of them were killed by firearms. One study found that domestic violence victims are five times more likely to be killed if their abuser has access to a gun.

An American woman is fatally shot by her partner every 16 hours.

Only 16 states can require suspected domestic violence offenders to surrender their firearms.

The Facts on Guns and Domestic Violence

Guns and domestic violence are a lethal combination, injuring and killing women every day in the United States. A gun is the weapon most commonly used in domestic homicides. In fact, more than three times as many women are murdered by guns used by their husbands or intimate acquaintances than are killed by strangers' guns, knives, or other weapons combined.

Contrary to many public perceptions, many women who are murdered are killed not by strangers but by men they know.

Nearly one-third of all women murdered in the United States in recent years were murdered by a current or former intimate partner. In 2000, 1,247 women, more than three a day, were killed by their intimate partners.

Of females killed with a firearm, almost two-thirds were killed by their intimate partners.

Access to firearms increases the risk of intimate partner homicide more than five times than in instances where there are no weapons, according to a recent study. In addition, abusers who possess guns tend to inflict the most severe abuse on their partners.

In 2002, 54 percent of female homicide victims were shot and killed with a gun.

Handguns are more likely than rifles or shotguns to be used in homicides in which men kill women. In 2002, handguns were used in 73 percent of cases where men used firearms to kill women.

In homicides where males use firearms to kill women, handguns are the most commonly used weapon, over rifles and shotguns. Seventy-three percent of all females were killed with a handgun.

In 1998, for every one woman who used a handgun to kill an intimate acquaintance in self-defense, 83 women were murdered by an intimate acquaintance using a handgun.

A study of women physically abused by current or former

intimate partners found a five-fold increased risk of the partner murdering the woman when the partner owned a gun.

Domestic violence misdemeanor convictions and restraining orders were the second most common reason for denials of handgun purchase applications between 1994 and 1998.

From 1998 to 2001, more than 2,800 people with misdemeanor domestic violence convictions were able to purchase guns without being identified by the National Instant Criminal Background Check System.

Source: https://www.thetrace.
org/2016/08/15-facts-that-show-how-guns-make-domestic-violence-even-deadlier/

About the Author

Sarah Gallardo, Founder of Sarah Speaks Up
Photo by Joelle Nawrocki

After surviving 10 years of domestic violence at the hands of her now ex-husband, Sarah vowed to help people who suffer the same fate.

The single mother stepped out of the shadows to become a certified domestic violence counselor.

She also founded Sarah Speaks Up, a nonprofit organization that works to support victims and survivors of domestic violence.

In addition to her counseling work, Sarah shares her story, and her poetry, in media interviews, at advocacy events, and with the local business community. She has spoken to the Women in Business Summit, A Toast to Women, Soroptimist Northeast Region Fall Conference, Take Back The Night, Prudence Crandall Center's Hope Breakfast, Prudence Crandall Center's Candlelight Vigil, Safe Futures Gala, West Hartford TV's "Talk of Our Times" and Todays Woman New England PBS.

Currently, Sarah is in the process of writing her second book, a compilation of stories from other survivors.

She is a living example that people can change their lives and flourish in the wake of domestic violence.

Before Sarah I was familiar with domestic violence and the broad impact it has on our society. Now I have a tool, this book, to help someone who is suffering in silence.

~ Kathleen Oyanadel

Domestic violence is not an issue relegated to a single gender. Women are victims. Men are victims. Children, elders, whole families, friends and neighbors bear the scars. Sarah Gallardo's *Hiding in Plain Sight* tells us this with agonizing reality. Very few books have as visceral an impact as *Hiding in Plain Sight*.

~ Gordon Hurlbert

This is a book that everyone should read! To travel along with Sarah on her journey is both eye-opening and life-changing. A heavy lesson that should be shared with every sister, mother, daughter, and friend.

~ Joanne Gustafson

This book touched me. Not being a survivor myself, it gave me an eye opening insight into DV and its shattering effects. What an incredible feat of raw strength to share one's story so others can know that there is help, support and love out there for them.

~ Susan Pizzolongo

To book Sarah Gallardo as a speaker,
email *sarahspeaksup@gmail.com* or visit sarahspeaksup.org.